THE SHYLOCK PLAY

Julia Pascal

THE SHYLOCK PLAY

An adaptation of William Shakespeare's
The Merchant of Venice

OBERON BOOKS
LONDON

First published in 2008 by Oberon Books Ltd
521 Caledonian Road, London N7 9RH
Tel: 020 7607 3637 / Fax: 020 7607 3629
e-mail: info@oberonbooks.com
www.oberonbooks.com

ISBN: 978-1-84002-812-6

Cover design by Andrzej Klimowski

Printed in Great Britain by CPI Antony Rowe, Chippenham.

Contents

For Ruth Posner who has inspired so much of my work

Preface by Dr Sonia Massai

Julia Pascal's *The Merchant of Venice* represents an important point of departure from late twentieth-century productions of this play, whose reception is inevitably linked to the problematic legacy of the Holocaust. Most original and inspired is Pascal's use of a new character called Sarah as a framing device. Sarah is a Holocaust survivor – played in the original production by Ruth Posner, a real-life survivor who escaped from the Warsaw Ghetto aged twelve. The play starts as Sarah is about to be shown around the Venetian ghetto. The tour never gets underway, because the water starts to rise and Sarah and her tour guide end up watching a stranded company of actors, who rehearse *The Merchant of Venice* then and there because they cannot get to their theatre. After this point, Sarah is seemingly marginalised by the mighty course of Shakespeare's play, speaking again only to urge Jessica to reconsider her decision to elope with Lorenzo and to become a Christian in scenes 13, 14 and 18, and to give a harrowing account of the sexual abuse she suffered while hiding in Poland in scene 15.[1]

Interestingly, Pascal was criticised both for going too far in rewriting Shakespeare and for not going far enough. However, Ruth/Sarah's self-conscious act of watching *The Merchant of Venice* is actually central to Pascal's revision of Shakespeare and effectively defuses one of the most problematic moments in the play, when Shylock whets his knife and prepares to carve a pound of flesh out of Antonio's bosom in the trial scene. Productions which humanise Shylock generate an unresolved tension between the trial scene and the rest of the play. As Richard Foulkes has noted, '[o]ne of the problems for a sophisticated Shylock, such as [Henry] Irving's and [Laurence] Olivier's, is the business with the knife and scales, which is implied in the text'.[2] Alternatively, productions which demonise Shylock have led members of

---

1   Other new scenes include a moving exchange between Shylock and Jessica (sc. 3) and new dialogue is interspersed to the Shakespearean original throughout, but most noticeably in the first scene set in Belmont (sc. 4), where Pascal offers her audience a liberated and outspoken Portia.

2   Richard Foulkes, 'Henry Irving and Laurence Olivier as Shylock', in *Theatre Notebook 27* (1973), 26-35, 33.

the audience to leave the theatre in shock and horror. Warren Chernaik, for example, reports walking out of Bill Alexander's 1987 production at the interval because he could not bear the prospect of watching 'a Shylock [Anthony Sher] fully capable of butchering Antonio in open court'.[3] Conversely, Pascal's use of Sarah as a framing device is mould-breaking for its power to challenge and neutralise the image of the knife-wielding Jew at the heart of the trial scene.

In Pascal's production, the stage in the trial scene is divided into two main areas: one taken up by the Duke, Bassanio and Gratiano, and later on by Portia and Nerissa; the other by Shylock and Antonio, who stand side by side opposite the Duke, by a group of Venetians right behind them, and by Jessica and Sarah, who sit in opposite corners on the outer edge of the stage, partly hidden by the Venetians. Adding Jessica and Sarah to the trial scene prevents the fictional space of the courtroom from being filled by Shylock's opponents, and, more importantly, transforms the fictional courtroom into a complex theatrical space, which in turn undermines the archetypal quality of Shylock's spectacular gesture.

The trial scene, when safely contained within the fictive bounds of Shakespeare's play, acquires the status of a powerful myth, or spectacle. In Pascal's production, Sarah and Jessica function both within and beyond the fictive boundaries of the courtroom and, in Sarah's case, also within and beyond the fictive boundaries of the framing device. Jessica, for example, is clearly sitting in the courtroom and her facial expression and body language suggest her horror as she watches her father turn into the stereotype of the blood-thirsty Jew seeking to take the life of a Christian, which Shakespeare borrowed from medieval legend.[4] However, when Shylock turns towards her as he approaches Antonio, he does not register her presence, thus suggesting that she is and is not there. Similarly, Sarah is simultaneously framing-device and part of the fictive world of Shakespeare's play, because she watches it

---

3   Warren Chernaik, *The Merchant of Venice, Writers and their Work* (Devon: Northcote House, 2005), 37.
4   A splendid study of how Jews were viewed by Shakespeare's contemporaries is James Shapiro, *Shakespeare and the Jews* (New York: Columbia University Press, 1996).

but she also interacts with the rehearsing actors, who respond to her without stepping out of character. Besides, the convergence of the biographical and the fictional in Sarah's character as played by Ruth Posner allows Ruth to remain visible both as Sarah and as Ruth throughout Pascal's production. In other words, Jessica's and Sarah's presence in this scene prevents the *theatrical* space from signifying as a unified *fictional* space. By layering the fictional space, Pascal produces a theatrical space which queers the gaze. The blurring of boundaries remarked upon by some reviewers is more accurately described as a fracturing of the field of vision into interconnected but ultimately separate, discrete categories – history and fiction – and separate, discrete temporal layers – the long history of European antisemitism, the recent ravages of the Holocaust, and the place of both in Pascal's and Posner's engagement with Shakespeare's text.

Sarah as a framing device is in turn contained within another layer of fiction. The opening stage direction in Pascal's version announces the following stage business: '*As audience come in AFRICANS lay out fake designer bags and sunglasses on sheets*'. This opening sequence connects the motif of slavery evoked by Shylock in the trial scene[5] to the rise of an economic system which would eventually produce the displacement and dispossession embodied by the African street sellers. Critical attention has often focused on the fact that the logic of exchange which informs the mercantile world inhabited by Shylock and the Venetians also applies to Belmont. The bond that grants Shylock the right to claim a pound of Antonio's flesh is mirrored by the lottery devised by Portia's father, which grants the suitor who chooses the casket containing her image the right to claim her hand and all that she has inherited from her father. Less attention has been devoted to the effects of the rise of a capitalist economy not only in terms of the commodification of labour (the Africans) but also in terms of the commodification of *all* agents involved in it, including those who benefit from the accumulation of capital.

---

5   Shylock pulls a black slave out of the crowd of Venetians watching the trial as he delivers the following lines, 'You have among you many a purchased slave / Which, like your asses and your dogs and mules, / You use in abject and in slavish parts / Because you bought them.' (sc. 21).

Antonio's melancholy in Shakespeare's opening scene is often interpreted as stemming from his homoerotic (or, in most recent productions, including Pascal's, openly homosexual) attachment to Bassanio. However, Pascal's use of the African sellers as yet another framing device grants unprecedented resonance to Salerio's theory that Antonio is melancholy because '[His] mind is tossing on the ocean'. Antonio, as much as the Africans, is commodified, dehumanised, and quite literally turned into his argosies, tossed on the ocean of Shylock's relentless fury, as described by Antonio in the trial scene: 'You may as well go stand upon the beach / And bid the main flood bate his usual height / … As seek to soften that,—than which what's harder? — / His Jewish heart'. Post-Holocaust productions of *The Merchant of Venice* tend to identify Shylock solely as the representative of a persecuted religious minority. Pascal's version is therefore all the more interesting because it offers a rare insight into Shylock as a scapegoat for both religious and economic anxieties associated with the rise of capitalism, the 'universal wolf' threatening to devour anything and anybody in its wake, including itself.[6]

When Sarah realizes that the actors are about to start rehearsing *The Merchant of Venice*, she makes the following remark: 'I know this. It's the Shylock play… I wish it had never been written'. Pascal expresses a similar view in her introduction to *Crossing Jerusalem*,[7] where she confesses how tired she is of seeing Shylock and Jessica as the major representatives of Jewishness on the English stage. It was however inevitable that Pascal, who had adapted Shakespeare before[8] and who has repeatedly explored post-war Jewish history through her work as director and playwright, would turn to *The Merchant of Venice*. And the result was a thought-provoking, radical production, which marked an important new stage in the afterlife of this play.

6   Ulysses in Shakespeare's *Troilus and Cressida* describes appetite as a 'universal wolf', which 'seconded with will and power, / Must make perforce an universal prey, / And last eat up himself' (1.3.122-5). These lines (quoted from Jonathan Bate and Eric Rasmussen, eds. William Shakespeare: Complete Works, the RSC Shakespeare, 2007) inspired Hugh Grady's seminal book, *Shakespeare's Universal Wolf: Studies in Early Modern Reification* (Oxford: Clarendon Press, 1996).

7   Julia Pascal, *Crossing Jerusalem, Year Zero, The Golem, St Joan* (London: Oberon, 2003).

8   *The Yiddish Queen Lear* (London: Oberon, 2001).

Introduction

The Merchant of Venice is the hardest Shakespearean drama for any Jew to watch. Today the central question is, did Shakespeare write a racist play or a play about racism? Is this a radical text advocating tolerance, with sympathies which extend far beyond Marlowe's *Jew of Malta*, or is it a mere reflection of Elizabethan antisemitism, tempered by two groundbreaking pleas for equality?

This ambiguity is what attracts both actors and audiences. With its themes of religious bigotry, money, trade, sex and women's defiance of male authority, the play is shockingly modern.

Nevertheless, at its heart, is the dangerous figure of 'The Jew'. Shylock has epitomised avarice, cruelty and vengeance since his first appearance in 1600. *To shylock* has become a verb meaning to extort or lend money at high interest because Shakespeare's Jew has long been the template of stereotypical 'Jewish behaviour' in the western imagination. It is no accident that Hitler loved it and had it produced often during the Third Reich.

Dr Susannah Heschel, writing in the *Harvard Theological Review* ('From Jesus to Shylock: Christian Supersessionism and *The Merchant of Venice*') describes a 1943 production organised by the SS Gauleiter Baldur von Schirach to celebrate the cleansing of Jews from Vienna:

'When Werner Krauss, the Nazis' leading actor, first appeared on stage as Shylock, he made the audience shudder. According to the newspaper account: With a crash and a weird train of shadows, something revoltingly alien and startlingly repulsive crawled across the stage… The pale pink face, surrounded by bright red hair and beard, with its unsteady, cunning little eyes; the greasy caftan with the yellow prayer shawl slung round; the splay-footed, shuffling walk; the foot stamping with rage; the claw-like gestures with the hands; the voice, now bawling, now muttering – all add up to a pathological image of the East European Jewish type.'

Since the Holocaust, few would dare depict Shylock as a *Der Stürmer* stereotype. Joel Berkowitz in his *Shakespeare on the*

American Yiddish Stage reveals that Yiddish companies have always had difficulties with the original text, which was often adapted to make it palatable to Jewish audiences. The play has never been a success in Israel.

Is the work so problematic for modern audiences because the figure of Shylock is just too disturbing? Before The Holocaust, Shylock was played on the English and European stage mainly as a hook-nosed, filthy outsider no doubt justified by Shakespeare's own Shylock, Richard Burbage, who performed the role in 1600 with a bright red wig and proboscis.

Arnold Wesker, whose play *The Merchant* challenged Shakespeare's vision, believes the character to be two-dimensional. 'He is malevolent from the start; possesses an evil imagination which conceives the pound of flesh bond, so miserly that he considers his recalcitrant daughter dead for marrying a Christian, so merciless that he cannot relent even when offered many times more the debt owed him. Many gentiles feel comfortable with such a portrait; it conforms to that image of the Jew with which they are most familiar'.

I believe Wesker's analysis to be correct but, however the play is adapted, there is still the central problem of Shakespeare's plot-device. Given that the Jewish law of *kashrut* forbids contact with blood, Shylock's demand for a pound of flesh is utterly implausible.

Nonetheless, the audience has to excuse Shakespeare's monumental error since, without it, there would be no motor to drive the play. Wesker's solution was to make the 'pound of flesh' deal a joke between the philosemitic Antonio and his friend Shylock. Mine has not been to change Shakespeare's text but to add to it. In my adaptation, there are two new prose scenes for Shylock and Jessica to show that, since the death of his wife, Shylock's only significant emotional relationship is with his daughter. She represents both his genetic and financial legacy.

Like Portia, she is wooed and won by a fortune-hunter but, whereas Portia enhances her status by marriage, Jessica wanders into the hostile wilderness of an antisemitic society. Although she believes conversion and marriage will bring assimilation, her brave new Christian world offers only exile from family, community and her own identity.

My 2007 production cast Paul Herzberg, a muscular, energetic actor in his early 50s. He played Shylock as a proud fighter pitting his wits against a virulent racist society. Rather than wearing a Jewish gabardine, he was dressed like all the other Venetians. The only thing that marked him out was his yarmulke. Otherwise he was a smart guy and a major player. The casting of Herzberg as an attractive man who refused to be victimised, was a vital element in this staging.

Equally important was the presence of Warsaw Ghetto survivor, Ruth Posner. She played Sarah, a contemporary visitor to the Venice Ghetto, who happens on a company of actors rehearsing *The Merchant of Venice*. The audience watch, Sarah, a survivor from the l942 Warsaw Ghetto, standing at the original sixteenth century Ghetto. It is a vision of Ghetto upon Ghetto, a framing device which poses difficult questions about the history of this text and its presentation. Sarah says, 'I know this. It's The Shylock Play. I wish it had never been written!' Her remark echoes the discomfort felt by so many Jews when confronting *The Merchant of Venice*.

We should not forget that the original title of the play on the 1600 quarto is *The most excellent Historie of the Merchant of Venice With the extreame crueltie of Shylocke the Jewe towards the sayd Merchant, in cutting a just pound of his flesh…*

This tells us that the dice are already loaded against Shylock. Although we now abbreviate the work as *The Merchant of Venice*, we know that Shakespeare had decided who was the good guy and who the bad, even before Shylock stepped onstage.

Julia Pascal
November 2008

Characters

ANTONIO, a merchant of Venice

BASSANIO, his friend and Portia's suitor

LEONARDO, Bassanio's servant

LORENZO GRAZIANO SALERIO SOLANIO,
all friends of Antonio and Bassanio

SHYLOCK, a Jew

JESSICA, his daughter

TUBAL, a Jew

LANCELOT, a clown, first Shylock's servant and
then Bassanio's

PORTIA, an heiress

NERISSA, her waiting-gentlewoman

BALTHASAR STEFANO,
Portia's servants

PRINCE OF MOROCCO

PRINCE OF ARAGON

DUKE OF VENICE

MAGNIFICOES OF VENICE

A jailer, attendants, and servants

CHARACTERS IN THE MODERN SECTION

SARAH, a Holocaust survivor

VALENTINA, an Italian guide

A group of actors who rehearse *The Merchant of
Venice* and play the following roles

Christian pilgrims

Carnival-goers

Church dignitiaries

Jews in The Ghetto

Two Africans selling bags and sunglasses

A prostitute

14

The first production of *The Shylock Play*, which was produced under Shakespeare's original title *The Merchant of Venice*, was on 11 September 2007 at the Arcola Theatre, London, with the following cast:

ANTONIO, a merchant of Venice, Rod Smith

BASSANIO, his friend and Portia's suitor, Jonathan Woolf

LEONARDO, Bassanio's servant, Giovanni Bienne

LORENZO, Tim Dewberry

GRAZIANO, James Baldwin

SALERIO, Simeon Perlin

SOLANIO, Marc Pickering

SHYLOCK, Paul Herzberg

JESSICA, his daughter, Jodie Taibi and Emily Sidonie

TUBAL a Jew, Tim Dewberry

LANCELOT, Rod Smith

PORTIA, Miranda Pleasence

NERISSA, Stephanie Brittain

PORTIA'S LOVER/BALTHASAR/STEFANO, Giovanni Bienne

PRINCE OF MOROCCO, Olalekan Lawal Jnr

PRINCE OF ARAGON, Marc Pickering

DUKE OF VENICE, Emily Sidonie/Marc Pickering

SARAH, Ruth Posner

VALENTINA, Judith Quin

INQUISITOR, Simeon Perlin

AFRICAN BAG SELLER, Tonderai Munyeva

AFRICAN SUNGLASSES SELLER, Olalekan Lawal Jnr

JAZZ SINGER, Emily Sidonie

VIOLINIST, Ruth Clarke-Irons

PROSTITUTE, Emmy Sainsbury

TRUMPETER, Zoe Walker

Director Julia Pascal

Designer Sam Boardman-Jacobs

Movement Director Thomas Kampe

Lighting Designer Tony Simpson

Musical Director Tony Brown

Graphic Designer Eugenie Dodd

Stage Manager Saskia Godwin

Consultant General Manager Susannah Kraft Levene

Act One

As audience come in AFRICANS lay out fake designer bags and sunglasses on sheets.

SELLER ONE: You want to buy a bag? Gucci? Prada? Chanel? Only the best here.

SELLER TWO: Don't buy his stuff. It's rubbish.

SELLER ONE: Get away from me you liar.

SELLER TWO: Ladies and gents. I've got sunglasses that will make you look like stars. From Hollywood to Bollywood. Look like a million dollars when you lounge around the Lido.

SELLER ONE: Don't buy from him. His bags. All stolen.

SELLER TWO: Liar. I'll kill you!

SELLER ONE: And he killed his mother too.

SELLER TWO: Don't listen to him. He's jealous. He wants to sell my sunglasses.

SELLER ONE: And his grandmother.

SELLER TWO: Even he can recognise class ladies and gentlemen. Look at his stuff compared to mine.

SELLER ONE: And his sister.

SELLER TWO: Can't even even give it away.

SELLER ONE: And his aunty.

SELLER TWO: Fake. All of it. It's not even real leather.

SELLER ONE: Who you calling 'fake'. Come over here and say that to me.

They look as if they are going to fight when a whistle sounds warning them to make a run for it as the police are on their way. They hurriedly stuff their wares into a sheet and run off.

Enter SARAH who looks around the Ghetto. Enter VALENTINA.

SARAH: (*In Italian.*) Scusi. Lei e la guida officiale?

VALENTINA: (*In English.*) Yes I am the official guide.

SARAH: (*To the audience.*) Why does everyone answer me in English?

VALENTINA: I have a PhD in Shakespeare's language. Why should I speak Italian?

SARAH: Will you show me around?

VALENTINA: You'll have to wait for the tour. Some people are joining the group. Five. Ten minutes. Have you got your ticket?

AMERICAN VOICE: (*Offstage.*) Hey I'm looking at gondolas and I don't hear anyone singing do you?

VALENTINA: Oh God. (*Pause.*) Where are you from?

SARAH: England.

VALENTINA: You don't sound it

SARAH: I was born in Poland.

VALENTINA: When did you leave?

Sound of Church Bells.

SARAH: After the war.

VALENTINA: Where were your parents?

SARAH: Will the tour start soon?

VALENTINA: I need the whole group here. It's not for individuals.

SARAH: Your English is good.

VALENTINA: Thank you.

SARAH: I still speak like a bloody foreigner.

VALENTINA: Was it hard for you to learn?

SARAH: At first. But who could I speak Polish to?

VALENTINA: You were in England all alone? When you were
a little girl?

SARAH: My aunt wanted to stay in Poland. She was a
Communist. My father was also a Communist.

VALENTINA: What happened to him?

SARAH: I never talk about it..

VALENTINA: Why?

SARAH: Who would believe me back then? And today? It's not
'fashionable'. (*Pause.*) I was in the Warsaw Ghetto. I made
a run for it. With my aunt. To the Aryan side.

VALENTINA: How old were you?

SARAH: Eleven. My father arranged for false papers and a
new identity. I pretended to be a Catholic. I knew the
words from school. 'Hail Mary full of grace, the Lord is
with thee'. I was a Jew who loved Mary and baby Jesus. I
loved the Church. It didn't love me.

VALENTINA: (*Ironic.*) Holy Mary mother of God

SARAH: Even the pope was friends with Hitler.

VALENTINA: And the one we've got now.

SARAH: My father was thirty-six when they took him. He
thought he was a Pole! He was in the Polish army. He
should have gone to Palestine.

VALENTINA: Palestine?

SARAH: He refused. He wasn't 'a Zionist'.

VALENTINA: Where did he go?

SARAH: Treblinka. (*Beat.*) And your family?

VALENTINA: The usual story. They loved the Church. And *Il Duce*. (*Pause.*) The group should be here but the water's rising and I don't know if there are any tables up for them to get across.

Sound of dog barking.

SARAH: Tell me about this place.

VALENTINA: The first ghetto was here in Venice. The word 'ghetto' comes from the Italian and means foundry because in this area metal was made. Italian and German Jews lived in the New Ghetto and Levantines in the Old Ghetto. Jews in Venice were segregated and taxed more heavily than anyone else. After 1516 they were forced to live on this island.

SARAH: How many synagogues are there ?

VALENTINA: The first you see here was for the Jews who came from Germany and the other synagogue was for those from Spain to escape the Inquisition. The only jobs they were permitted was money-lending, they could be doctors and they could sell furniture or old clothes. If they left the Ghetto they had to wear a red or yellow hat or a yellow patch over their heart.

SARAH: I wore a yellow star.

VALENTINA: Yes.

SARAH: On the way here I saw some people with masks.

VALENTINA: Tomorrow is Good Friday. Some people they do carnival all through the year.

SARAH: Why do you do this job?

VALENTINA: It's a job.

SARAH: Yes but seeing Jews here day after day. Don't you get sick of it?

VALENTINA: Sick of it? (*She doesn't know what to say.*) You know they always ask me if I'm Jewish.

SARAH: Americans?

VALENTINA: Usually yes.

SARAH: Yes. Does that bother you?

VALENTINA: Yesterday there was an elderly man. A Jew who had been a GI. He'd liberated Italy. Well not on his own of course. That's why I do the job. A Jewish American who freed us from the Fascists while my grandparents were Fascists who did god-knows-what. (*A little lost she returns to her 'tourist speech'.*) Did you know that the Jews could leave this Ghetto during the day and work in Venice. But at six o'clock they had to be behind the walls. Behind the gate. Then they were cut off from the rest of the world and forced into this small space. There were hundreds of them living in cramped quarters.

SARAH: We were nineteen to a room in the Warsaw Ghetto. (*Silence.*) How many Jews are there in Italy today?

VALENTINA: Not many.

SARAH: You Italians, what do you say about Jews now?

VALENTINA: 'Big noses.' 'Good with money.'

A group of actors come onstage with costumes, tables and chairs. Following actors' lines taken according to action.

VALENTINA: (*In Italian.*) What are you doing?

ACTOR: Inglese?

VALENTINA: What are you doing?

ACTOR: We're rehearsing a play. Well it's a dress rehearsal.

VALENTINA: Here?

ACTOR: (*Thinks she hasn't understood.*) The dress rehearsal!

ACTOR: What's wrong?

VALENTINA: A play here?

ACTOR: Why not?

VALENTINA: Do you have permission?

ACTOR: You kidding?

VALENTINA: You can't perform here. I'm waiting for a group.

ACTOR 1: The flooding's started. Nobody can get through. Your group is stranded.

ACTOR 2: Even our director's caught. Let's run through anyway.

ACTOR 3: This place is cool. The Ghetto used to be a gamblers' paradise. And there was music here. Just like in Harlem in the thirties.

ACTOR 4: Come on Antonio. (*They have set up a café scene.*) (*To SARAH.*) Hey you! You want to watch?

SARAH: Oh yes.

SCENE TWO

ACTOR: Come on Antonio.

ANTONIO: In sooth, I know not why I am so sad.
　　It wearies me, you say it wearies you,
　　But how I caught it, found it, or came by it,
　　What stuff 'tis made of, whereof it is born,
　　I am to learn;
　　And such a want-wit sadness makes of me
　　That I have much ado to know myself.

SALERIO: Your mind is tossing on the ocean,
　　There where your argosies with portly sail,
　　Like signors and rich burghers on the flood—

Or as it were the pageants of the sea—
Do overpeer the petty traffickers
That curtsy to them, do them reverence,
As they fly by them with their woven wings.

SOLANIO: (*To Antonio*.) Believe me, sir, had I such venture forth
　　The better part of my affections would
　　Be with my hopes abroad. I should be still
　　Plucking the grass to know where sits the wind,
　　Peering in maps for ports and piers and roads,
　　And every object that might make me fear
　　Misfortune to my ventures out of doubt
　　Would make me sad.

SALERIO:　　　　　　　　My wind cooling my broth
　　Would blow me to an ague when I thought
　　What harm a wind too great might do at sea.
　　I should not see the sandy hour-glass run
　　But I should think of swallows and of flats,
　　And see my wealthy Andrew, decks in sand,
　　Wailing her hightop lower than her ribs
　　To kiss her burial. Should I go to church
　　And see the holy edifice of stone
　　And not bethink me straight of dangerous rocks
　　Which, touching but my gentle vessel's side,
　　Would scatter all her spices on the stream,
　　Enrobe the roaring waters with my silks,
　　And, in a word, but even now worth this,
　　And now worth nothing? Shall I have the thought
　　To think on this, and shall I lack the thought
　　That such a thing bechanced would make me sad?
　　But tell not me. I know Antonio
　　Is sad to think upon his merchandise.

ANTONIO: Believe me, no. I thank my fortune for it,
　　My ventures are not in one bottom trusted,
　　Nor to one place; nor is my whole estate
　　Upon the fortune of this present year.
　　Therefore my merchandise makes me not sad.

SOLANIO: Why then, you are in love.

ANTONIO: Fie, fie.

SOLANIO: Not in love neither? Then let us say you are sad
    Because you are not merry, and 'twere as easy
    For you to laugh, and leap, and say you are merry
    Because you are not sad. Now, by two-headed Janus,
    Nature hath framed strange fellows in her time:
    Some that will evermore peep through their eyes
    And laugh like parrots at a bagpiper,
    And other of such vinegar aspect
    That they'll not show their teeth in way of smile.

Enter BASSANIO, LORENZO, and GRAZIANO.

    Here comes Bassanio, your most noble kinsman,
    Graziano, and Lorenzo. Fare ye well.
    We leave you now with better company.

SALERIO: I would have stayed till I had made you merry
    If worthier friends had not prevented me.

ANTONIO: Your worth is very dear in my regard.
    I take it your own business calls on you,
    And you embrace th'occasion to depart.

SALERIO and SOLANIO leave.

LORENZO: My lord Bassanio, since you have found Antonio,
    We two will leave you; but at dinner-time
    I pray you have in mind where we must meet.

BASSANIO: I will not fail you.

GRAZIANO: You look not well, Signor Antonio.
    You have too much respect upon the world.
    They lose it that do buy it with much care.
    Believe me, you are marvellously changed.

ANTONIO: I hold the world but as the world, Graziano—
    A stage where every man must play a part,
    And mine a sad one.

GRAZIANO: Come, good Lorenzo.—Fare ye well a while.
　　I'll end my exhortation after dinner.
　　Lorenzo (*To ANTONIO and BASSANIO.*) Well, we will leave
　　　you
　　Then till dinner-time.

GRAZIANO and LORENZO leave.

ANTONIO caresses BASSANIO. It is clear they are lovers.

ANTONIO: Well, tell me now what lady is the same
　　To whom you swore a secret pilgrimage,
　　That you do today promised to tell me of.

BASSANIO: 'Tis not unknown to you, Antonio,
　　How much I have disabled mine estate
　　By something showing a more swelling port
　　Than my faint means would grant continuance,
　　Nor do I now make moan to be abridged
　　From such a noble rate; but my chief care
　　Is to come fairly off from the great debts
　　Wherein my time, something too prodigal,
　　Hath left me gag'd. To you, Antonio,
　　I owe the most in money and in love,
　　And from your love I have a warranty
　　To unburden all my plots and purposes
　　How to get clear of all the debts I owe.

ANTONIO: I pray you, good Bassanio, let me know it,
　　And if it stand as you yourself still do,
　　Within the eye of honour, be assured
　　My purse, my person, my extremest means
　　Lie all unlocked to your occasions.

BASSANIO: In my schooldays, when I had lost one shaft,
　　I shot his fellow of the selfsame flight
　　The selfsame way, with more advised watch
　　To find the other forth; and by adventuring both,
　　I oft found both. I urge this childhood proof
　　Because what follows is pure innocence.
　　I owe you much, and, like a willful youth,

That which I owe is lost; but if you please
To shoot another arrow that self way
Which you did shoot the first, I do not doubt
As I will watch the aim, or to find both
Or bring your latter hazard back again,
And thankfully rest debtor for the first.

ANTONIO: You know me well, and herein spend but time
To wind about my love with circumstance;
And out of doubt you do me now more wrong
In making question of my uttermost
Than if you had made waste of all I have.
Then do but say to me what I should do
That in your knowledge may by me be done.
And I am pressed unto it. Therefore speak.

BASSANIO: In Belmont is a lady richly left
And she is fair, and, fairer than that word,
Of wondrous virtues. Sometimes from her eyes
I did receive fair speechless messages.
Her name is Portia, nothing undervalued
To Cato's daughter, Brutus' Portia;
Nor is the wide world ignorant of her worth,
For the four winds blow in from every coast
Renowned suitors, and her sunny locks
Hang on her temples like a golden fleece,
Which makes her seat of Belmont Colchis' strand,
And many Jasons come in quest of her.
O my Antonio, had I but the means
To hold a rival place with one of them,
I have a mind presages me such thrift
That I should questionless be fortunate.

ANTONIO: Thou know'st that all my fortunes are at sea,
Neither have I money nor commodity
To raise a present sum. Therefore go forth—
Try what my credit can in Venice do;
That shall be racked even to the uttermost
To furnish thee to Belmont, to fair Portia.
Go presently enquire, and so will I,

Where money is; and I no question make
To have it of my trust or for my sake.

Exeunt.

SARAH: I know this. It's the Shylock Play!

VALENTINA: Shakespeare stole it from the Italian story. *Il Pecorone.* The Jew who makes a loan against a pound of flesh.

SARAH: I wish it had never been written.

TABLEAU

Catholic mass. The ensemble becomes a religious procession.

CHANTING: Misericordia. A statue of The Virgin is carried.

JESSICA is following a line of PRIESTS and NUNS.

They don't see her. A NUN is praying.

JESSICA is fascinated. SARAH prays with her.

SCENE THREE

JESSICA lights the sabbath candles. She covers her head.

SHYLOCK breaks a bit of Challah bread, eats a little and gives her some. He pours wine in a goblet for both of them. They clink glasses and say L'chaim. He hugs her hard.

JESSICA: Shabbat shalom.

SHYLOCK: Shabbat Shalom (*Kisses her. They sit. He blesses the wine. They clink glasses.*) L'chaim.

JESSICA: L'chaim.

SHYLOCK: My 'Gitelle.' (*They sit.*)

JESSICA: What did you call me?

SHYLOCK: It's your Jewish name. 'The good one.'

JESSICA: I may not live up to that.

SHYLOCK: Your mother Leah was named after Jacob's wife.

JESSICA: But Jacob didn't want her, he was in love with her prettier, younger sister, Rachel.

SHYLOCK: You remember.

JESSICA: And Jacob had to work seven hard years for nothing to get Rachel.

SHYLOCK: Indeed.

JESSICA: The bible is full of cheats. Why do you always quote it?

SHYLOCK: It's how you learn.

JESSICA: King David kills a man so that he can steal his wife. Adultery, lies and murder. That's the bible. That's what we come from!

SHYLOCK: Enough! I am talking about your mother, Leah. The only woman I ever wanted.

JESSICA: Ten years she's been dead. Ten years!

SHYLOCK: And every night I reach out to her empty space in my bed.

JESSICA: Why don't you take another wife?

SHYLOCK: I don't want another wife. All I have in the world is you.

Silence.

JESSICA: I am hungry. Shall we eat?

SCENE FOUR

PORTIA is lying on a daybed, covered in a sheet.

PORTIA: By my troth, Nerissa, my little body is aweary of this great world.

NERISSA: You would be, sweet madam, if your miseries were in the same abundance as your good fortunes are.

A young lover crawls out from under PORTIA's cover.

PORTIA: Good sentences, and well pronounced.

NERISSA: They would be better if well followed.

PORTIA: The brain may devise laws for the blood, but a hot temper leaps o'er a cold decree.
There is this painting. Titan's Venus. She is naked with her hand just here. (*Over her vagina.*) It is known as a wedding picture but she is with no man.

LOVER: My favourite is Lotto Lorenzo's Venus and Cupid.

PORTIA: Why?

LOVER: Cupid angelically pissing through a wreath of roses and petals scattered all over her 'there'.

PORTIA: Why?

LOVER: He's deflowering her!

PORTIA: Ah you are so good for my education! But this reasoning is not in the fashion to choose me a husband. 'Choose'! I may neither choose who I would nor refuse who I dislike; so is the will of a living daughter curbed by the will of a dead father.

NERISSA: Your father was ever virtuous, and holy men at their death have good inspirations; therefore the lottery that he hath devised in these three chests of gold, silver, and lead, whereof who chooses his meaning chooses you, will no doubt never be chosen by any rightly but one who you shall rightly love.
First there is the Neapolitan prince. Then is there the County Palatine. What say you then to Falconbridge, the young baron of England? What think you of the Scottish lord, his neighbour? How like you the young German, the Duke of Saxony's nephew?

PORTIA: Very vilely in the morning when he is sober, and
most vilely in the afternoon when he is drunk.
I will do anything, Nerissa, ere I will be married to a
sponge.

NERISSA: Relax. They've all gone home. Nobody wanted to
risk losing your father's test.

PORTIA: Sweet words. Let's throw a party! I'm learning salsa!
(*She dances sexily.*)
(*Tongue in cheek.*) If I live to be as old as Sibylla I will die
as chaste as Diana.

NERISSA: Unless you are won through your father's will.
Do you remember, a certain Venetian, a scholar and a
soldier?

PORTIA: Bassanio, the spendthrift.

NERISSA: Bassanio the beautiful.

PORTIA: I remember him well.

PORTIA: But whoever I marry he will have all that I own.
And I will be his servant. Suppose we close the gates to
all these suitors. What then? (*There is the sound of banging
on the door.*) Why are they banging on the doors to come
in? My father leaves me to bounty hunters. Don't answer.
Don't answer.

A dog barks. LANCELOT with a noose runs across the stage.

LANCELOT: Where's that cur? I'll hang him. I'll throttle him,
I'll hang him from the highest tree

TABLEAU

*Cast are drumming. Crossover movement scene. GRAZIANO watches
JESSICA. He makes a sexual gesture towards her. She runs away
in fear.*

SCENE FIVE
A Café

SHYLOCK: Three thousand ducats. Well.

BASSANIO: Ay, sir, for three months.

SHYLOCK: Three months, well.

BASSANIO: For the which, as I told you, Antonio shall be
bound.

SHYLOCK: Antonio shall become bound. Well.

BASSANIO: May you stead me? Will you pleasure me? Shall I
know your answer?

SHYLOCK: Three thousand ducats for three months, and
Antonio bound.

BASSANIO: Your answer to that.

SHYLOCK: Antonio is a good man.

BASSANIO: Have you heard any imputation to the contrary?

SHYLOCK: Ho, no, no, no, no! My meaning in saying he is
a good man is to have you understand me that he is
sufficient. Yet his means are in supposition. He hath
an argosy bound to Tripolis, another to the Indies. I
understand moreover upon the Rialto he hath a third at
Mexico, a fourth for England, and other ventures he hath
squandered abroad. But ships are but boards, sailors but
men. There be land rats and water rats, water thieves and
land thieves—I mean pirates—and then there is the peril
of waters, winds, and rocks. The man is, notwithstanding,
sufficient. Three thousand ducats. I think I may take
his bond.

BASSANIO: Be assured you may.

SHYLOCK: I will be assured I may, and that I may be assured,
I will bethink me. May I speak to Antonio?

BASSANIO: If it please you to dine with us.

SHYLOCK: Yes, to smell pork, to eat of the habitation which
your prophet the Nazarite conjured the devil into! I will
buy with you, sell with you, talk with you, walk with you,
and so following, but I will not eat with you, drink with
you, nor pray with you. What news on the Rialto?
(*Enter ANTONIO.*) Who is he comes here?

BASSANIO: This is Signor Antonio.

SHYLOCK: (*Aside.*) How like a fawning publican he looks.
I hate him for he is Christian;
But more, for that in low simplicity
He lends out money gratis, and brings down
The rate of usance here with us in Venice.
If I can catch him once upon the hip
I will feed fat the ancient grudge I bear him.
He hates our sacred nation, and he rails,
Even there where merchants most do congregate,
On me, my bargains, and my well-won thrift—
Which he calls interest. Cursed be my tribe
If I forgive him.

BASSANIO: Shylock, do you hear?

SHYLOCK: I am debating of my present store,
And by the near guess of my memory
I cannot instantly raise up the gross
Of full three thousand ducats. What of that?
Tubal, a wealthy Hebrew of my tribe,
Will furnish me. But soft—how many months
Do you desire? (*To ANTONIO.*) Rest you fair, good signor.
Your worship was the last man in our mouths.

SHYLOCK extends his hand. ANTONIO ignores it.

ANTONIO: Shylock, albeit I neither lend nor borrow
By taking nor by giving of excess,
Yet to supply the ripe wants of my friend
I'll break a custom. (*To BASSANIO.*) Is he yet possessed
How much ye would?

SHYLOCK: Ay, ay, three thousand ducats.

ANTONIO: And for three months.

SHYLOCK: I had forgot—three months. You told me so.—
    Well then, your bond; and let me see—but hear you,
    Methoughts you said you neither lend nor borrow
    Upon advantage.

ANTONIO: I do never use it.

SHYLOCK: When Jacob grazed his uncle Laban's sheep—
    This Jacob from our holy Abram was,
    As his wise mother wrought in his behalf,
    The third possessor; ay, he was the third—

ANTONIO: And what of him? Did he take interest?

SHYLOCK: No, not take interest, not, as you would say,
    Directly int'rest. Mark what Jacob did:
    When Laban and himself were compromised
    That all the eanlings which were streaked and pied
    Should fall as Jacob's hire, the ewes, being rank,
    In end of autumn turned to the rams,
    And when the work of generation was
    Between these woolly breeders in the act,
    The skilful shepherd peeled me certain wands,
    And in the doing of the deed of kind
    He stuck them up before the fulsome ewes
    Who, then conceiving, did in eaning time.
    Fall parti-coloured lambs; and those were Jacob's.
    This was a way to thrive; and he was blest;
    And thrift is blessing, if men steal it not.

ANTONIO: This was a venture, sir, that Jacob served for—
    A thing not in his power to bring to pass,
    But swayed and fashioned by the hand of heaven.
    Was this inserted to make interest good,
    Or is your gold and silver ewes and rams?

SHYLOCK: I cannot tell. I make it breed as fast. But note me,
    signor—

ANTONIO: Mark you this, Bassanio?

The devil can cite Scripture for his purpose.
An evil soul producing holy witness
Is like a villain with a smiling cheek,
A goodly apple rotten at the heart.
O, what a goodly outside falsehood hath!

SHYLOCK: Three thousand ducats. 'Tis a good round sum.
Three months from twelve—then let me see the rate.

ANTONIO: Well, Shylock, shall we be beholden to you?

SHYLOCK: Signor Antonio, many a time and oft
In the Rialto you have rated me
About my moneys and my usances.
Still have I borne it with a patient shrug,
For suff'rance is the badge of all our tribe.
You call me misbeliever, cut-throat, dog,
And spit upon my Jewish gaberdine,
And all for use of that which is mine own.
Well then, it now appears you need my help.
Go to, then. You come to me, and you say
'Shylock, we would have moneys'—you say so,
You, that did void your rheum upon my beard,
And foot me as you spurn a stranger cur
Over your threshold. Moneys is your suit.
What should I say to you? Should I not say
'Hath a dog money? Is it possible
A cur can lend three thousand ducats?' Or
Shall I bend low, and in a bondsman's key,
With bated breath and whisp'ring humbleness
Say this: 'Fair sir, you spat on me on Wednesday last;
You spurned me such a day; another time
You called me dog; and for these courtesies
I'll lend you thus much moneys'?

ANTONIO: I am as like to call thee so again,
To spit on thee again, to spurn thee too.
If thou wilt lend this money, lend it not
As to thy friends; for when did friendship take
A breed for barren metal of his friend?

But lend it rather to thine enemy,
Who if he break, thou mayst with better face
Exact the penalty.

SHYLOCK: Why, look you, how you storm!
I would be friends with you, and have your love,
Forget the shames that you have stained me with,
Supply your present wants, and take no doit
Of usance for my moneys and you'll not hear me.
This is kind I offer.

BASSANIO: This were kindness.

SHYLOCK: This kindness will I show.
Go with me to a notary, seal me there
Your single bond, and, in a merry sport,
If you repay me not on such a day,
In such a place, such sum or sums as are
Expressed in the condition, let the forfeit
Be nominated for an equal pound
of your fair flesh to be cut off and taken
In what part of your body pleaseth me.

BASSANIO: You shall not seal to such a bond for me.
I'd rather dwell in my necessity.

ANTONIO: Why, fear not, man; I will not forfeit it.
Within these two months—that's a month before
This bond expires—I do expect return
Of thrice three times the value of this bond.

SHYLOCK: O father Abram, what these Christians are,
Whose own hard dealings teaches them suspect
The thoughts of others! Pray you tell me this:
If he should break his day, what should I gain
By the extraction of the forfeiture?
A pound of man's flesh taken from a man
Is not so estimable, profitable neither,
As to flesh of muttons, beefs, or goats. I say,
To buy his favour I extend this friendship.
If he will take it, so. If not, adieu,

And, for my love, I pray you wrong me not.

ANTONIO: Yes, Shylock, I will seal unto this bond.

SHYLOCK: Then meet me forthwith at a notary's.
　　Give him directions for this merry bond,
　　And I will go and purse the ducats straight,
　　See to my house—left in the fearful guard
　　Of an unthrifty knave—and presently
　　I'll be with you.

Exit SHYLOCK.

ANTONIO:　　　　　Hie thee, Gentle Jew.
　　The Hebrew will turn Christian; he grows kind.

BASSANIO: I like not fair terms, and a villain's mind.

ANTONIO: Come on. In this there can be no dismay.
　　My ships come home a month before the day.

SCENE SIX

Enter PRINCE OF MOROCCO, with PORTIA and NERISSA and their train.

MOROCCO: Mislike me not for my complexion,
　　The shadowed livery of the burnished sun,
　　To whom I am a neighbour and near bred.
　　Bring me the fairest creature northward born
　　Where Phoebus' fire scarce thaws the icicles
　　And let us make incision for your love
　　To prove whose blood is reddest, his or mine
　　I tell thee, lady, this aspect of mine
　　Hath feared the valiant. By my love I swear,
　　The best regarded virgins of our clime
　　Have loved it too. I would not change this hue
　　Except to steal your thoughts, my gentle queen.

PORTIA: In terms of choice I am not solely led
　　By nice direction of a maiden's eyes.
　　Besides, the lott'ry of my destiny

Bars me the right of voluntary choosing.
You must take your chance,
And either not attempt to choose at all,
Or swear before you choose, if you choose wrong
Never to speak to lady afterward
In way of marriage. Therefore be advised.

MOROCCO: Nor will not. Come, bring me unto my chance.

PORTIA: First, forward to the temple. After dinner
Your hazard shall be made.

MOROCCO: Good fortunes then,
To make me blest or cursed'st among men.

SCENE SEVEN
The Street

LANCELOT: Certainly my conscience will serve me to run
from this Jew my master. This fiend is at mine elbow
tempts me, saying to me saying to me 'Gobbo, Lancelot
Gobbo, good Lancelot or good Gobbo' or 'good Lancelot
Gobbo, use your legs, take the start, run away.' My
conscience says, 'No, take heed, honest Lancelot, take
heed, honest Gobbo or as aforesaid honest Lancelot
Gobbo—do not run scorn running with thy heels'. Well
the most courageous fiend bids me 'pack, for the heavens
rouse up a brave mind', says the fiend, 'and run'. Well
my conscience hanging about the neck of my heart says
very wisely to me: 'My honest friend Launcelot'—being
an honest man's son, or rather an honest woman's son,
for indeed my father did something, smack, something
grow into, he had a kind of taste, well my conscience says
'Launcelot budge not!'
'Budge!' says the fiend.
'Budge not', says my conscience. 'Conscience' say I,
'you counsel well',—'Fiend', say I, 'you counsel well'.
To be ruled by my conscience I should stay with the Jew
my master who (God bless the mark), is a kind of devil;
and to run away from the Jew I should be ruled by the

fiend who, (saving your reverence) is the devil himself. Certainly the Jew is the very devil incarnation; and in my conscience, my conscience is but a kind of hard conscience to offer counsel me to stay with the Jew. The fiend gives the more friendly counsel. 'I will run, fiend. My master's a very Jew. Give him a present?—give the wolf a halter!'

(*He swings a rope.*) I am famished in his service. You may tell every finger I have with my ribs. Give me your present to one Master Bassanio. If I serve not him, I will run as far as God has any ground.

Enter BASSANIO with LEONARDO and Followers.

Here comes the man. To him, for I am a Jew if I serve the Jew any longer.

BASSANIO: Wouldst thou aught with me?

LANCELOT: (*To BASSANIO.*) Indeed, the short and long is, I serve the Jew, and have a desire.

BASSANIO: What would you?

LANCELOT: Serve you, sir.

BASSANIO: I know thee well. Thou hast obtained thy suit.
Shylock the master spoke with me this day,
And hath preferred thee, if it be preferment
To leave a rich Jew's service to become
The follower of so poor a gentleman.

LANCELOT: I'll take my leave of the Jew in the twinkling.

Exit

BASSANIO: I pray thee, good Leonardo, think on this.
These things being bought and orderly bestowed,
Return in haste, for I do feast tonight
My best-esteemed acquaintance. Hie thee. Go.

Enter GRAZIANO.

LEONARDO: My best endeavours shall be done herein.

GRAZIANO: Signor Bassanio.

BASSANIO: Graziano.

GRAZIANO: I have a suit to you.

BASSANIO: You have obtained it

GRAZIANO: You must not deny me. I must go with you to
    Belmont.

BASSANIO: Why then, you must. But hear thee, Graziano,
    Thou art too wild, too rude and bold of voice—
    Parts that become thee happily enough,
    And in such eyes as ours appear not faults;
    But where thou art not known, why, there they show
    Something too liberal. Pray thee, take pain
    To allay with some cold drops of modesty
    Thy skipping spirit, lest through thy wild behaviour
    I be misconstered in the place I go to,
    And lose my hopes.

GRAZIANO: Signor Bassanio, hear me.
    If I do not put on a sober habit,
    Talk with respect, and swear but now and then,
    Wear prayer books in my pocket, look demurely—
    Nay more, while grace is saying hood mine eyes
    Thus with my hat, and sigh, and say 'Amen',
    Use all the observance of civility,
    Like one well studied in a sad ostent
    To please his grandam, never trust me more.

BASSANIO: Well, we shall see your bearing.

GRAZIANO: Nay, but I bar tonight. You shall not gauge me
    By what we do tonight.

BASSANIO: No, that were pity.
    I would entreat you rather to put on
    Your boldest suit of mirth, for we have friends
    That purpose merriment. But fare you well.
    I have some business.

GRAZIANO: And I must visit Lorenzo and the rest.
But we will visit you at supper-time.

TABLEAU

JESSICA is sitting on the roof of SHYLOCK's house in the Ghetto. She remembers the stories of the Inquisition but this is also a representation of current forced conversion. There is a double level theatrically.

Group sequence witnessed by JESSICA.

Using movement, the cast represent people escaping from the Inquisition. They perform both the victims and the torturers. Sound of dog noises. This is also a reference to the fact that dogs and wolves were hanged in the seventeenth century and the double resonance that Jews are often referred to as dogs in The Merchant of Venice.

Crossfade to SHYLOCK pulling JESSICA's hair out of a cap to bleach it in the sun. He squeezes lemons over it.

SCENE EIGHT

JESSICA: Someone is hanging dogs again. How long does it take to die? A big dog probably takes the longest but that depends on its weight and the skill of the hangman. Have you thought of that?

SHYLOCK: Do you have to talk about this?

JESSICA: The worst is a wolf. He yelps when it goes wrong. The noise stays in me for hours. (*Beat.*) Why did mother die?

SHYLOCK: She wanted to give me a son.

JESSICA: Isn't a daughter enough?

Small pause.

SHYLOCK: Why are you so beautiful?

JESSICA: Am I?

SHYLOCK: You'll have your head turned and leave me.

JESSICA: Do you think there's enough lemon?

SHYLOCK: Who knows what boys run after you?

JESSICA: Nobody.

SHYLOCK: Gentiles?

JESSICA: No.

SHYLOCK: What happens when I leave this house?

JESSICA: Enough!

SHYLOCK: When I am out, who comes knocking?

JESSICA: Mind that doesn't get in my eye!

SHYLOCK: I used to sing you to sleep, do you remember?

JESSICA: And when I woke in the morning you were gone.

SHYLOCK: Your mother needed me.

JESSICA: You could have stayed.

SHYLOCK: Leah gave me a ring. It's all I have of her. Do you
    want it? A turquoise.

JESSICA: Oh yes! (*He removes the ring. It is hard to remove. He yells
    as it comes off.*) You sound like the devil.

SHYLOCK: Jessica!
    Since my wedding day I have never taken off this ring. I
    love you Jessica. More than my life. Do you know that?
    More than my life.

JESSICA: More lemon. Blonder. Blonder.

SCENE NINE
Shylock's house

Carnival noises in the distance.

JESSICA: I am sorry thou wilt leave my father so.
    Our house is hell, and thou, a merry devil,

Didst rob it of some taste of tediousness.
But fare thee well. There is a ducat for thee.
And, Lancelot, soon at supper shalt thou see
Lorenzo, who is thy new master's guest.
Give him this letter, do it secretly;
And so farewell. I would not have my father
See me in talk with thee.

LANCELOT: Adieu. Tears exhibit my tongue, most beautiful
pagan; most sweet Jew; if a Christian do not play the
knave and get thee, I am much deceived. But adieu.
These foolish drops do something drown my manly spirit.
Adieu.

JESSICA: Farewell, good Lancelot.
Alack, what heinous sin is it in me
To be ashamed to be my father's child!
But though I am a daughter to his blood,
I am not to his manners. O Lorenzo,
If thou keep promise I shall end this strife,
Become a Christian and thy loving wife.

SCENE TEN
St Mark's Square

The water level is very high and everyone has to cross on tables. There are people dancing to a forties jazz band. JESSICA is watching. ANTONIO dances with BASSANIO. SHYLOCK sees nobody in his haste to get back.

Enter GRAZIANO, LORENZO, SALERIO and SOLANIO.

LORENZO has the PROSTITUTE with him. The other men start to flirt with her. LORENZO pushes them away.

LORENZO: Nay, we will slink away in supper-time,
Disguise us at my lodging, and return
All in an hour.

GRAZIANO: We have not made good preparation.

SALERIO: We have not spoke as yet of torchbearers.

SOLANIO: 'Tis vile, unless it may be quaintly ordered,
    And better in my mind not undertook.

LORENZO: 'Tis now but four o'clock. We have two hours
    To furnish us—

Enter LANCELOT with a letter.

    Friend Lancelot, what's the news?

GRAZIANO: Love-news, in faith.

LANCELOT: By your leave, sir.

LORENZO: Whither goest thou?

LANCELOT: Marry, sir, to bid my old master the Jew to sup
    tonight with my new master the Christian.

LORENZO: Hold, here, take this. (*Giving money.*) Tell gentle
    Jessica
    I will not fail her. Speak it privately.
    Go.
    Gentlemen,
    Will you prepare you for this masque tonight?
    I am provided of a torchbearer.

SALERIO: Ay, marry, I'll be gone about it straight.

SOLANIO: And so will I.

LORENZO: Meet me and Graziano
    At Graziano's lodging some hour hence.

SALERIO: 'Tis good we do so.

GRAZIANO: Was not that letter from fair Jessica?

LORENZO: I must needs tell thee all. She hath directed
    How I shall take her from her father's house,
    What gold and jewels she is furnished with,
    What page's suit she hath in readiness.
    If e'er the Jew her father come to heaven
    It will be for his gentle daughter's sake;
    And never dare misfortune cross her foot

Unless she do it under this excuse:
That she is issue to a faithless Jew.
Come, go with me. Use as thou go.
Fair Jessica shall be my torchbearer.

GRAZIANO takes the PROSTITUTE from LORENZO.

SCENE ELEVEN
Shylock's House

SHYLOCK is hemming JESSICA's coat.

JESSICA is coming home from across the Venice bridges. Music.

SHYLOCK: Well, thou shalt see, thy eyes shall be thy judge,
The difference of old Shylock and Bassanio.
What, Jessica! Thou shall not gourmandise
As thou has done with me. What, Jessica!
And sleep and snore and rend apparel out.
Why, Jessica, I say!

LANCELOT: Why, Jessica!

SHYLOCK: Who bids thee call? I do not bid thee call.

LANCELOT: Your worship was wont to tell me I could do
nothing without bidding.

JESSICA arrives flushed and guilty.

JESSICA: Call you? What is your will?

He gives her the coat. She puts it on.

SHYLOCK: I am bid forth to supper, Jessica.
These are my keys. But wherefore should I go?
I am not bid for love. They flatter me,
But yet I'll go in hate, to feed upon
The prodigal Christian. Jessica, my girl,
Look to my house. I am right loath to go.
There is some ill a-brewing towards my rest,
For I did dream of money-bags tonight.

The hem is the correct length. SHYLOCK kisses her, sits and pulls her onto his knee.

LANCELOT: I beseech you, sir, go. My young master doth
    expect your reproach.

SHYLOCK: So I do his.

LANCELOT: And they have conspired together. I will not
    say you shall see a masque, this day before Easter, but
    if you do, then it was not for nothing that my nose fell
    a-bleeding on Black Monday last at six o'clock i'th'
    morning, falling out that year on Ash Wednesday was
    four year in th' afternoon.

SHYLOCK: What, are there masques? Here you me, Jessica,
    Lock up my doors; and when you hear the drum
    And the vile squealing of the wry-necked fife,
    Clamber not you up to the casements then,
    Nor thrust your head into the public street
    To gaze on Christian fools with varnished faces,
    But stop my house's ears—I mean my casements.
    Let not the sound of shallow fopp'ry enter
    My sober house. By Jacob's staff I swear
    I have no mind of feasting forth tonight.

JESSICA: Stay!

SHYLOCK: But I will go.

JESSICA: Father!

SHYLOCK: Go you before me, sirrah.
    Say I will come.

LANCELOT: I will go before, sir. (*Aside to JESSICA.*)
    Mistress, look out at windows for all this.
    There will come a Christian by
    Will be worth a Jewess' eye.

SHYLOCK: What says that fool of Hagar's offspring, ha?

JESSICA: His words were 'Farewell, mistress,' nothing else.

SHYLOCK: The patch is kind enough, but a huge feeder.
Well, Jessica, go in.
Perhaps I will return immediately.
Do as I bid you. Shut doors after you.
Fast bind, fast find—
A proverb never stale in thrifty mind.

JESSICA: Farewell; and if my fortune be not crossed,
I have a father, you a daughter lost.

SARAH: I have a father, you a daughter lost.
Don't go!

JESSICA: Who are you?

SARAH: Your mother.

JESSICA: No you're not.

SARAH: I could be.

JESSICA: My grandmother?

SARAH: If you like.

JESSICA: What do you want of me?

SARAH: Stay. He needs you.

JESSICA: Leave me alone you old witch.

SCENE TWELVE
The street

Enter masquers, GRAZIANO, and SALERIO.

They find SARAH onstage and taunt her using the long nose on the Venetian masque to make antisemitic gestures. SARAH runs from them.

GRAZIANO: This is the penthouse under which Lorenzo
Desired us to make stand.

SALERIO: His hour is almost past.

GRAZIANO: And it is marvel he outdwells his hour,

For lovers ever run before the clock.

SALERIO: O, ten times faster Venus' pigeons fly
　　To seal love's bonds new made than they are wont
　　To keep obliged faith unforfeited.

GRAZIANO: That ever holds. Who riseth from a feast
　　With that keen appetite that he sits down?
　　Where is the horse that doth untread again
　　His tedious measures with the unabated fire
　　That he did pace them first? All things that are
　　Are with more spirit chased than enjoyed.
　　How like a younker or a prodigal
　　The scarfed barque puts from her native bay,
　　Hugged and embraced by the strumpet wind!
　　How like the prodigal doth she return,
　　With over-weathered ribs and ragged sails,
　　Lean, rent, and beggared by the strumpet wind!

　　Enter LORENZO.

SALERIO: Here comes Lorenzo. More of this hereafter.

LORENZO: Sweet friends, your patience for my long abode.
　　Not I but my affairs have made you wait.
　　When you shall please to play the thieves for wives
　　I'll wait as long for you therein.

　　SARAH enters and goes to JESSICA.

JESSICA: Get away from me!

SARAH: He wants your money.

JESSICA: He wants me.

SARAH: That's what you think.

JESSICA: You have no idea.

SARAH: Don't marry.

JESSICA: What?

SARAH: When your father dies you'll have all you need.

JESSICA: I don't want his gold.

SARAH: Well you won't get it. Your husband takes all.
     You're his meal ticket.

JESSICA: I don't care.

SARAH: He's not faithful to you even now!

JESSICA: You're lying. You're jealous.

SARAH: Don't forget my words.

LORENZO: Approach.
     Here dwells my father Jew. Ho, who's within?

JESSICA: Who are you? Tell me for more certainty,
     Albeit I'll swear that I do know your tongue.

LORENZO: Lorenzo, and thy love.

JESSICA: Lorenzo, certain, and my love indeed.
     For who love I so much? And now who knows
     But you, Lorenzo, whether I am yours?

LORENZO: Heaven and thy thoughts are witness that thou art.

JESSICA: Here, catch this casket.

SARAH: Jessica!

JESSICA: It is worth the pains.
     I am glad 'tis night, you do not look on me.
     For I am much ashamed of my exchange,
     But love is blind, and lovers cannot see
     The pretty follies that themselves commit;
     For it they could, Cupid himself would blush
     To see me thus transformed to a boy.

LORENZO: Descend, for you must be my torchbearer.

JESSICA: What, must I hold a candle to my shames?
     They in themselves, good sooth, are too too light.
     Why, 'tis an office of discovery, love,
     And I should be obscured.

LORENZO: So are you, sweet,
 Even in the lovely garnish of a boy.
 But come at once,
 For the close night doth play the runaway,
 And we are stayed for at Bassanio's feast.

JESSICA: I will make fast the doors, and gild myself
 With some more ducats, and be with you straight.

               Exit.

GRAZIANO: Now, by my hood, a gentile, and no Jew.

LORENZO: (*Caressing the money.*)
 Beshrew me but I love her heartily,
 For she is wise, if I can judge of her;
 And fair she is, if that mine eyes be true;
 And therefore like herself, wise, fair, and true,
 Shall she be placed in my constant soul.

 Enter JESSICA.

  What, art thou come? On, gentlemen, away.
 Our masquing mates by this time for us stay.

               Exit.

 Enter ANTONIO.

ANTONIO: Who's there?

GRAZIANO: Signor Antonio?

ANTONIO: Fie, fie, Graziano, where are all the rest.
 'Tis nine o'clock. Our friends all stay for you.
 No masque tonight. The wind is come about.
 Bassanio presently will go aboard.
 I have sent twenty out to seek for you.

GRAZIANO: I am glad on't. I desire no more delight.
 Than to be under sail and gone tonight.

SCENE THIRTEEN – PROLOGUE

SARAH: There was a man.

JESSICA: What man?

SARAH: When I was in hiding. In Warsaw. He was fat. And old. His belly was huge.

JESSICA: Why are you telling me this?

SARAH: He waits 'til my aunt goes out.

JESSICA: My Lorenzo is a god.

SARAH: Alone in the bedroom. He is watching me. Holy Mary Mother of God pray for us sinners—

JESSICA: Virgin Mother that's what he says. Now and at the hour of

SARAH / JESSICA: our death.

JESSICA: Am I a sinner to leave my father? But oh I want Lorenzo. If I don't have him I will die.

SARAH: This man. His wife is outside milking the cow. What happens if she comes in?

JESSICA: I have to keep secret—

SARAH: It's our secret he says as he opens his lips. Black stumps—

JESSICA: and his smell it is salt.

SARAH: his mouth all wet and he puts his big tongue in my mouth. His hands between my legs.

JESSICA: No man has ever touched me. Except my father.

SARAH: 'Little girl I can show you paradise!'

JESSICA: Why do I shake when my love is near me?

SARAH: Where is my father why can't he save me?

JESSICA: Lorenzo lifts my hair and tells me I have 'Jewish ears'. Why does he say that?

SARAH: I tell my aunt. She says we must run. There are silver rings hidden in the skirt of my coat. My father put them there to bribe the peasants. But when the silver is gone who will hide us?

JESSICA: And he lifts my skirt and tells me I have Jewish feet. But my body's like any other girl's. Isn't it?

SARAH: Run! Run! Run! Fire falls from the sky. Run! Someone's coming.

JESSICA: Suppose I go there and he hates me?

SARAH: Soldiers. In a different uniform. They play jazz from loudspeakers. They have jeeps. There's a black man. Smiling. He's holding something for me to take. I put it in my mouth. It's sweet.

JESSICA: Lorenzo. He won't hate me. He'll love me. Forever. Won't he?

SCENE THIRTEEN
Belmont

PORTIA, ARAGON and MOROCCO.

PORTIA: Draw aside the curtains and discover the several caskets. The one of them contains my picture, prince. If you choose that, then I am yours withal.

MOROCCO: This first of gold, who this inscription bears;
'Who chooseth me shall gain what many men desire.'
The second silver, which this promise carries:
'Who chooseth me shall get as much as he deserves.'
This third dull lead, with warning all as blunt
'Who chooseth me, must give and hazard all he hath.'
How shall I know if I do choose the right?

PORTIA: (*To ARAGON.*) Behold there stands the caskets noble prince.

> If you choose that wherein I am contained
> Straight shall our nuptial rites be solemnised.

ARAGON: I am enjoin'd by oath never to unfold to any one
Which casket 'twas I chose;
And so have I address'd me,—fortune now
to my heart's hope!

PORTIA: Now make your choice.

MOROCCO: Some God direct my judgment! Let me see,
I will survey th'inscriptions back again, —

MOROCCO / ARAGON: What says this leaden casket?
'Who chooseth me must give and hazard all he hath.'

MOROCCO: Must give, for what?

ARAGON: For lead?

MOROCCO: Hazard for lead?Men that hazard all do it in hope
of fair advantages. A golden mind stoops not to shows of
dross. I'll then nor give nor hazard aught for lead.

ARAGON: I will not choose what many men desire,
Because I will not jump with common spirits
And rank me with the barbarous multitudes.
Why then, to thee, thou silver treasure-house.

MOROCCO: What says the silver with her virgin hue?
'Who chooseth me shall get as much as he deserves.'
As much as I deserve—why, that's the lady!
What if I strayed no farther, but chose here?
Let's see once more this saying grav'd in gold.

MOROCCO reaches for the gold casket.

ARAGON reaches for the silver casket.

PORTIA: There, take it, Prince; and if my form lie there, then I
am yours.

MOROCCO: 'Who chooseth me shall gain what many
men desire.'

ARAGON: 'Who chooseth me shall have as much as
    he deserves.'

MOROCCO: O hell! What have we here?

ARAGON: Did I deserve no more than a fool's head?
    Is that my prize? Are my deserts no better?

MOROCCO: A carrion death, within whose empty eye
    There is a written scroll. I'll read the writing.
    'All that glisters is not gold;
    Fare you well; your suit is cold.'

ARAGON: With one fool's head I came to woo,
    But I go away with two.

Exit.

MOROCCO: Portia, adieu. I have too grieved a heart
    To take a tedious leave. Thus losers part.

Exit.

PORTIA: (*Crosses herself with relief.*) Let all of his complexion
    choose me so.

*As PORTIA and her entourage leave, GRAZIANO is waiting onstage.
He wants to attack Jews returning to the Ghetto. SHYLOCK crosses the
street. GRAZIANO pushes him to start a fight. He expects SHYLOCK
to cower and is shocked to receive a punch. SHYLOCK walks off and
the furious GRAZIANO looks for someone else to harass. He sees the
AFRICAN SELLER sitting on the floor waiting for customers and
kicks him in the face.*

SCENE FOURTEEN
On the Rialto Bridge

Enter SALERIO and SOLANIO.

SALERIO: Why, man, I saw Bassanio under sail.
    With him is Graziano gone alone,
    And in their ship I am sure Lorenzo is not.

SOLANIO: The villain Jew with outcries raised the Duke,
Who went with him to search Bassanio's ship.

SALERIO: He came too late. The ship was under sail.
But there the Duke was given to understand
That in a gondola were seen together
Lorenzo and his amorous Jessica.
Besides, Antonio certified the Duke
They were not with Bassanio in his ship.

SOLANIO: I never heard a passion so confused,
So strange, outrageous, and so variable.
As the dog Jew did utter in the streets.
'My daughter! O, my ducats! O, my daughter!
Fled with a Christian! O, my Christian ducats!
Justice! The law! My ducats and my daughter!
A sealed bag, two sealed bags of ducats,
Of double ducats, stol'n from me by my daughter!
And jewels, two stones, two rich and precious stones,
Stol'n by my daughter! Justice! Find the girl!
She hath the stones upon her, and the ducats!'

SALERIO: Why, all the boys in Venice follow him
Crying, 'His stones, his daughter, and his ducats!'

SOLANIO: Let good Antonio look he keep his day,
Or he shall pay for this.

SALERIO: Marry, well remembered.
I reasoned with a Frenchman yesterday,
Who told me in the narrow seas that part
The French and English there miscarried
A vessel of our country, richly fraught.
I thought upon Antonio when he told me,
And wished in silence that it were not his.

SOLANIO: You were best to tell Antonio what you hear—
Yet do not suddenly, for it may grieve him.

SALERIO: A kinder gentleman treads not the earth.
I saw Bassanio and Antonio part.
Bassanio told him he would make some speed

Of his return. He answered, 'Do not so.
Slubber not business for my sake, Bassanio,
But stay the very riping of the time;
And for the Jew's bond which he hath of me,
Let it not enter your mind of love.
Be merry, and employ your chiefest thoughts
To courtship and such fair ostents of love
As shall conveniently become you there.'
And even there, his eye being big with tears,
Turning his face, he put his hand behind him
And, with affection wondrous sensible,
He wrung Bassanio's hand; and so they parted.

SOLANIO: I think he only loves the world for him.
I pray thee let us go and find him out,
And quicken his embraced heaviness
With some delight or other.

SALERIO: Do we so.

Musical interlude from jazz singer. All actors onstage to have a musical jam. (Scat music) Water Rising.

ACTOR : (*To SARAH.*) This is where we have our break. You want a glass of something?

Interval.

ACT TWO

SCENE FIFTEEN
The Rialto

SOLANIO: Now, what news on the Rialto?

SALERIO: Why, yet it lives there unchecked that Antonio hath a ship of rich lading wrecked on the narrow seas—the Good-wins I think they call the place—a very dangerous flat, and fatal, where the carcasses of many a tall ship lie buried, as they say, if my gossip report be an honest woman of her word.

SOLANIO: I would she were as lying a gossip in that as ever knapped ginger or made her neighbours believe she wept for the death of a third husband. But it is true, without any slips of prolixity or crossing the plain highway of talk, that the good Antonio, the honest Antonio—o that I had a title good enough to keep his name company—

SALERIO: Come, the full stop.

SOLANIO: Why, the end is he hath lost a ship.

SALERIO: I would it might prove the end of his losses.

SOLANIO: Let me say amen betimes, lest the devil cross my prayer.For here is comes in the likeness of a Jew.
How now, Shylock, What news among the merchants?

SHYLOCK: You knew, none so well, none so well as you, of my daughter's flight.

SALERIO: That's certain. I for my part knew the tailor that made the wings she flew withal.

SOLANIO: And Shylock for his own part knew the bird was fledge, and then it is the complexion of them all to leave the dam.

SHYLOCK: She is damned for it.

SALERIO: That's certain, if the devil may be her judge.

SHYLOCK: My own flesh and blood to rebel!

SOLANIO: Out upon it, old carrion, rebels it at these years?

SHYLOCK: I say my daughter is my flesh and my blood.

SALERIO: There is more difference between thy flesh and hers than between jet and ivory; more between your bloods than there is between red wine and Rhenish. But tell us, do you hear whether Antonio have had any loss at sea or no?

SHYLOCK: There I have another bad match. A bankrupt, a prodigal, who dare scarce show his head on the Rialto; a beggar, that was used to come so smug upon the mart. Let him look to his bond. He was wont to lend money for a Christian courtesy: let him look to his bond.

SALERIO: Why, I am sure if he forfeit thou wilt not take his flesh. What's that good for?

SHYLOCK: To bait fish withal. If it will feed nothing else it will feed my revenge. He hath disgraced me, and hindered me half a million; laughed at my losses, mocked at my gains, scorned my nation, thwarted my bargains, cooled my friends, heated mine enemies, and what's his reason?—I am a Jew. Hath not a Jew eyes? Hath not a Jew hands, organs, dimensions, senses, affections, passions; fed with the same food, hurt with the same weapons, subject to the same diseases, healed by the same means, warmed and cooled by the same winter and summer as a Christian is? If you prick us, do we not bleed? If you tickle us do we not laugh? If you poison us, do we not die? And if you wrong us shall we not revenge? If we are like you in the rest, we will resemble you in that. If a Jew wrong a Christian, what is his humility? Revenge. If a Christian wrong a Jew, what should his sufferance be by Christian example? Why, revenge. The villainy you teach me I will execute, and it shall go hard but I will better the instruction.

MAN: (*From ANTONIO.*) Gentlemen, my master Antonio is at his house and desire to speak with you both.

SALERIO: We have been up and down to seek him.

Enter TUBAL.

SOLANIO: Here comes another of the tribe. A third cannot be matched unless the devil himself turn Jew.

Exit.

SHYLOCK: How now, Tubal? What news from Genoa? Hast thou found my daughter?

TUBAL: I often came where I did hear of her, but cannot find her.

SHYLOCK: Why, there, there, there, there. A diamond gone cost me two thousand ducats in Frankfurt. The curse never fell upon our nation till now—I never felt it till now. Two thousand ducats in that and other precious, precious jewels. I would my daughter were dead at my foot and the jewels in her ear! Would she were hearsed at my foot and the ducats in her coffin! No news of them? Why, so. And I know not what's spent in the search. Why thou, loss upon loss; the thief gone with so much, and so much to find the thief, and no satisfaction, no revenge, nor no ill luck stirring but what lights o' my shoulders, no sighs but o'my breathing, no tears but o' my shedding.

TUBAL: Yes, other men have ill luck too. Antonio, as I heard in Genoa—

SHYLOCK: What, what, what? Ill luck, ill luck?

TUBAL: Hath an argosy cast away coming from Tripolis.

SHYLOCK: I thank God, I thank God! Is it true, is it true?

TUBAL: I spoke with some of the sailors that escaped the wreck.

SHYLOCK: I thank thee, good Tubal. Good news, good news! Ha, ha—heard you in Genoa?

TUBAL: Your daughter spent in Genoa, as I heard, one night fourscore ducats.

SHYLOCK: Thou stick'st a dagger in me. I shall never see my gold again. Fourscore ducats at a sitting? Fourscore ducats?

TUBAL: There came divers of Antonio's creditors in my company to Venice that swear he cannot choose but break.

SHYLOCK: I am very glad of it. I'll plague him, I'll torture him. I am glad of it.

TUBAL: One of them showed me a ring that he had of your daughter for a monkey.

SHYLOCK: Out upon her! Thou torturest me, Tubal. It was my turquoise. I had it of Leah when I was a bachelor. I would not have given it for a wilderness of monkeys.

TUBAL: But Antonio is certainly undone.

SHYLOCK: Nay, that's true, that's very true. Go, Tubal, fee me an officer. Bespeak him a fortnight before. I will have the heart of him if he forfeit, for were he out of Venice I can make what merchandise I will. Go, Tubal, and meet me at our synagogue. Go, good Tubal; at our synagogue, Tubal.

Jessica. My Jessica. My ring. My Leah. For a monkey?

He says kaddish.

TUBAL: Why do you say kaddish for her. Jessica is not dead.

SHYLOCK: She is to me.

SCENE SIXTEEN

Split scene.

The conversion of JESSICA.

And the wooing of PORTIA.

PORTIA dances for BASSANIO. JESSICA is walking in procession behind THE INQUISITOR.

PORTIA: (*To BASSANIO.*) I pray you tarry. Pause a day or two
    Before you hazard, for in choosing wrong
    I lose your company.

INQUISITOR: Do you renounce the devil?

JESSICA: I do.

INQUISITOR: Do you accept the blood of Christ?

SARAH: Don't do that!

JESSICA: Get away from me.

PORTIA: Therefore forbear a while.
    There's something tells me—but it is not love—
    I would not lose you; and you know yourself
    Hate counsels not in such a quality.
    But lest you should not understand me well—
    And yet a maiden hath no tongue but thought—
    I would detain you here some month or two
    Before you venture for me.

INQUISITOR: The blood of Christ. Do you accept it Jewess?

PORTIA: I could teach you
    How to choose right, but then I am forsworn.
    So will I never be; so may you miss me.
    But if you do, you'll make me wish a sin,
    That I had been forsworn. Beshrew your eyes,
    They have o'erlooked me and divided me.
    One half of me is yours, the other half yours—

    Mine own, I would say, but if mine, then yours,
    And so all yours.

JESSICA: I accept Christ

SARAH: Don't betray your father. You are all he has.

INQUISITOR: Do you accept his blood?

JESSICA: Shut up about my father will you?

PORTIA: O, these naughty times
    Puts bars between the owners and their rights;
    And so, though yours, not yours. Prove it so,
    Let fortune go to hell for it, not I.
    I speak too long, but tis to piece the time,
    To eke it, and to draw it out in length
    To stay you from election.

BASSANIO: Let me choose,
    For as I am, I live upon the rack.

PORTIA: Upon the rack, Bassanio? Then confess
    What treason there is mingled with your love.

BASSANIO: None but that ugly treason of mistrust
    Which makes me fear th'enjoying of my love.
    There may as well be amity and life
    'Tween snow and fire as treason and my love.

MAN: Do you accept Christ's blood?

JESSICA: A Jew will not touch blood.

MAN: But you are not a Jew. Accept Jesus!

PORTIA: Ay, but I fear you speak upon the rack,
    Where men enforced do speak anything,

BASSANIO: Promise me life and I'll confess the truth.

PORTIA: Well then, confess and live.

BASSANIO: 'Confess and love'
    Had been the very sum of my confession.

O happy torment, when my torturer
. Doth teach me answers for deliverance!
But let me to my fortune and the caskets.

PORTIA: Away then. I am locked in one of them.
If you do love me, you will find me out.
Nerissa and the rest, stand all aloof.
Let music sound while he doth make his choice.

JESSICA sings Ave Maria.

BASSANIO: What find I here?
'You that choose not by the view
Chance as fair and choose as true.
Since this fortune falls to you,
Be content and seek no new.
If you be well pleased with this,
And hold your fortune for your bliss,
Turn you where your lady is,
And claim her with a loving kiss.'

PORTIA: But now I was the lord
Of this fair mansion, master of my servants,
Queen o'er myself; and even now, but now,
This house, these servants, and this same myself
Are yours, my lord's. I give them with this ring,
Which when you part from, lose, or give away,
Let it presage the ruin of your love,
And be my vantage to exclaim on you.

INQUISITOR: Do you reject Satan and all his works and all his
empty promises?

JESSICA: I do!

INQUISITOR: We anoint you with the oil of salvation in the
name of Christ who reigns for ever and ever.

*JESSICA falls slowly to the floor in ecstasy and religious fervour.
BASSANIO and PORTIA kiss.*

BASSANIO: Madam, you have bereft me of all words.

Only my blood speaks to you in my veins,
And there is such confusion in my powers
As after some oration fairly spoke
By a beloved prince there doth appear
Among the bussing pleased multitude,
Where every something being blent together
Turns to a wild of nothing save of joy,
Expressed and not expressed. But when this ring
Parts from this finger, then parts life from hence.
O, then be bold to say Bassanio's dead.

Exit JESSICA.

NERISSA: My lord and lady, it is now our time
That have stood by and seen our wishes prosper
To cry 'Good joy, good joy, my lord and lady!'

GRAZIANO: My lord Bassanio, and my gentle lady,
I wish you all the joy that you can wish,
For I am sure you can wish none from me.
And when your honours mean to solemnize
The bargain of your faith, I do beseech you
Even at that time I may be married too.

BASSANIO: With all my heart, so thou canst get a wife.

GRAZIANO: I thank you lordship, you have got me one.
My eyes, my lord, can look as swift as yours.
You saw the mistress, I beheld the maid.
I got a promise of this fair one here
To have her love, provided that your fortune
Achieved her mistress.

PORTIA: Is this true, Nerissa?

NERISSA: Madam, it is, so you stand pleased withal.

BASSANIO: And do you, Graziano, mean good faith?

GRAZIANO: Yes, faith, my lord.

BASSANIO: Our feast shall be much honoured in your
marriage.

GRAZIANO: We'll play with them the first boy for a thousand
ducats.

PORTIA: (*To the audience.*) The first boy. Why do they always
want a boy?

NERISSA: What, and stake down?

GRAZIANO: No, we shall ne'er win that sport and stake down.
But who comes here? Lorenzo and his infidel!
What, and my old Venetian friend Salerio!

*Enter LORENZO, SALERIO. JESSICA now has a large crucifix around
her neck. She wears a blonde wig as a symbol of assimilation. It
should look natural.*

BASSANIO: Lorenzo and Salerio, welcome hither,
if that the youth of my new int'rest here
Have power to bid you welcome. By your leave,
I bid my very friends and countrymen,
Sweet Portia, welcome

PORTIA: So do I, my lord. They are entirely welcome.

LORENZO: I thank your honour. For my part, my lord,
My purpose was not to have seen you here,
But meeting with Salerio by the way
He did entreat me past all saying nay
To come with him along.

SALERIO: I did, my lord,
And I have reason for it. Signor Antonio
Commends him to you.

BASSANIO: Ere I ope his letter
I pray you tell me how my good friend doth.

SALERIO: Not sick, my lord, unless it be in the mind;
Nor well, unless in mind. His letter there
Will show you his estate.

GRAZIANO: Nerissa, cheer yon stranger. Bid her welcome.

JESSICA is only greeted by NERISSA and rather coldly.

> Your hand, Salerio. What's the news from Venice?
> How doth that royal merchant good Antonio?
> I know he will be glad of our success.
> We are the Jasons; we have won the fleece.

SALERIO: I would you had won the fleece that he hath lost.

PORTIA: There are some shrewd contents in yon same paper
> That steals the colour from Bassanio's cheek.
> Some dear friend dead, else nothing in the world
> Could turn so much the constitution
> Of any constant man. What, worse and worse?
> With leave, Bassanio, I am half yourself,
> And I must freely have the half of anything
> That this same paper brings you.

BASSANIO: O sweet Portia,
> Here are a few of the unpleasant'st words
> That ever blotted paper. Gentle lady,
> When I did first impart my love to you
> I freely told you all the wealth I had
> Ran in my veins: I was a gentleman;
> And then I told you true; and yet, dear lady,
> Rating myself at nothing, you shall see
> How much I was a braggart. When I told you
> My state was nothing, I should then have told you
> That I was worse than nothing, for indeed
> I have engaged myself to a dear friend,
> Engaged my friend to his mere enemy,
> To feed my means. Here is a letter, lady,
> The paper as the body of my friend,
> And every word in it a gaping wound
> Issuing life-blood. But is it true, Salerio?
> Hath all his ventures failed? What, not one hit?
> From Tripolis, from Mexico, and England,
> From Lisbon, Barbary, and India,
> And not one vessel scape the dreadful touch
> Of merchant-marring rocks?

SALERIO: Not one, my lord.

Besides, it should appear that if he had
The present money to discharge the Jew
He would not take it. Never did I know
A creature that did bear the shape of a man
So keen and greedy to confound a man.
He plies the Duke at morning and night,
And doth impeach the freedom of the state
If they deny him justice. Twenty merchants,
The duke himself, and the magnificoes
Of greatest port, have all persuaded with him,
But none can drive him from the envious plea
Of forfeiture, of justice, and his bond.

JESSICA: When I was with him I have heard him swear
To Tubal and to Cush, his countrymen,
That he would rather have Antonio's flesh
Than twenty times the value of the sum
That he did owe him; and I know, my lord,
If law, authority, and power deny him not,
It will go hard with poor Antonio.

PORTIA: Is it your dear friend that is thus in trouble?

BASSANIO: The dearest friend to me, the kindest man,
The best-conditioned and unwearied spirit
In doing courtesies, and one in whom
The ancient Roman honour more appears
Than any that draws breath in Italy.

PORTIA: What sum owes he the Jew?

BASSANIO: For me, three thousand ducats.

PORTIA: What, no more?
Pay him six thousand and deface the bond.
Double six thousand, and then treble that,
Before a friend of this description
Shall lose a hair through Bassanio's fault.
First go with me to church and call me wife,
And then away to Venice to your friend;
For never shall you lie by Portia's side

With an unquiet soul. You shall have gold
To pay the petty debt twenty times over.
When it is paid, bring your true friend along.
My maid Nerissa and myself meantime
Will live as maids and widows. Come, away,
For you shall hence upon your wedding day.
Bid your friends welcome, show a merry cheer.
Since you are dear bought, I will love you dear.
But let me hear the letter of your friend.

BASSANIO: 'Sweet Bassanio, my ships have all miscarried, my
creditors grow cruel, my estate is very low, my bond to
the Jew is forfeit, and since in paying it, it is impossible I
should live, all debts are cleared between you and I if I
might but see you at my death. Notwithstanding, use your
pleasure. If your love do not persuade you to come, let
not my letter.'

PORTIA: O, love! Dispatch all business, and be gone.

BASSANIO: Since I have your good leave to go away
I will make haste, but till I come again
No bed shall e'er be guilty of my stay
Nor rest be interposer 'twixt us twain.

SCENE SEVENTEEN

Enter SHYLOCK, SOLANIO, ANTONIO, and the jailer.

SHYLOCK: Jailer, look to him. Tell not me of mercy.
This is the fool that lent out money gratis.
Jailer, look to him.

ANTONIO: Hear me yet, good Shylock.

SHYLOCK: I'll have my bond. Speak not against my bond.
I have sworn an oath that I will have my bond.
Thou called'st me dog before thou hadst a cause,
But since I am a dog, beware my fangs.
The Duke shall grant me justice. I do wonder,

Thou naughty jailer, that thou are so fond
To come abroad with him at his request.

ANTONIO: I pray thee hear me speak.

SHYLOCK: I'll have my bond. I will not hear thee speak.
I'll have my bond, and therefore speak no more.
I'll not be made a soft and dull-eyed fool
To shake the head, relent, and sigh, and yield
To Christian intercessors. Follow not.
I'll have no speaking. I will have my bond.

SOLANIO: It is the most impenetrable cur
That ever kept with men.

ANTONIO: Let him alone.
I'll follow him no more with bootless prayers.
He seeks my life. His reason well I know:
I oft delivered from his forfeitures
Many that have at times made moan to me.
Therefore he hates me.

SOLANIO: I am sure the Duke
Will never grant this forfeiture to hold.

ANTONIO: The Duke cannot deny the course of law,
For the commodity that strangers have
With us in Venice, if it be denied,
Will much impeach the justice of the state.
Since that the trade and profit of the city
Consisteth of all nations. Therefore go,
These griefs and losses have so bated me
That I shall hardly spare a pound of flesh
Tomorrow to my bloody creditor.
Well, jailer, on. Pray God Bassanio come
To see me pay his debt, and then I care not.

SCENE EIGHTEEN

Enter PORTIA, NERISSA, LORENZO, JESSICA and BALTHAZAR (a man of PORTIA's).

LORENZO: Madam, although I speak it in your presence,
    You have a noble and a true conceit
    Of godlike amity, which appears most strongly
    In bearing thus the absence of your lord.
    But if you knew to whom you show this honour,
    How true a gentleman you send relief,
    How dear a lover of my lord your husband,
    I know you would be prouder of the work
    Than customary bounty can enforce you.

PORTIA: I never did repent for doing good,
    Nor shall not now; for in companions
    That do converse and waste the time together,
    Whose souls do bear and equal yoke of love,
    There must be needs a like proportion
    Of lineaments, of manners, and of spirit,
    Which makes me think that this Antonio,
    Being the bosom lover of my lord,
    Must needs be like my lord. If it be so,
    How little is the cost I have bestowed
    In purchasing the semblance of my soul
    From out the state of hellish cruelty.
    This comes too near the praising of myself,
    Therefore no more of it. Hear other things:
    Lorenzo, I commit into your hands
    The husbandry and manage of my house
    Until my lord's return. For mine own part,
    I have toward heaven breathed a secret vow
    To live in prayer and contemplation,
    Only attended by Nerissa here,
    Until her husband and my lord's return.
    There is a monastery two miles off,
    And there we will abide. I do desire you
    Not to deny this imposition,

The which my love and some necessity
Now lays upon you.

LORENZO: Madam, with all my heart,
I shall obey you in all fair commands.

PORTIA: My people do already know my mind,
And will acknowledge you and Jessica
In place of Lord Bassanio and myself.
So fare you well till we shall meet again.

LORENZO: Fair thoughts and happy hours attend on you!

JESSICA: I wish your ladyship all heart's content.

PORTIA: I thank you for your wish, and am well pleased
To wish it back on you. Fare you well, Jessica.
Now, Balthasar,
As I have ever found thee honest-true,
So let me find thee still. Take this same letter,
And use thou all th'endeavour of a man
In speed to Padua. See thou render this
Into my cousin's hands, Doctor Bellario,
And look what notes and garments he doth give thee,
Bring them, I pray thee, with imagined speed
Unto the traject, to the common ferry
Which trades to Venice. Waste no time in words,
But get thee gone. I shall be there before thee.

BALTHASAR: Madam, I go with all convenient speed.

PORTIA: Come on, Nerissa. I have work in hand
That you yet know not of. We'll see our husbands
Before they think of us.

NERISSA: Shall they see us?

PORTIA: They shall, Nerissa, but in such a habit
That they shall think we are accomplished
With that we lack

NERISSA: Why, shall we turn to men?

SCENE NINETEEN
The Trial

Procession and music.

Enter the DUKE, the magnificoes, ANTONIO, BASSANIO, GRAZIANO and SALERIO. (JESSICA and SARAH watch throughout and are seen by the audience. In the Court Room the crowd taunt and jeer SHYLOCK.)

DUKE: What, is Antonio here?

ANTONIO: Ready, so please your grace.

DUKE: I am sorry for thee. Thou art come to answer
    A stony adversary, an inhuman wretch
    Uncapable of pity, void and empty
    From any dram of mercy.

ANTONIO: I have heard
    Your grace hath ta'en great pains to qualify
    His rigorous course, but since he stands obdurate,
    And that no lawful means can carry me
    Out of his envy's reach, I do oppose
    My patience to his fury, and am armed
    To suffer with a quietness of spirit
    The very tyranny and rage of his.

DUKE: Go one, and call the Jew into the court.

SALERIO: He is ready at the door. He comes, my lord.

    Enter SHYLOCK.

DUKE: Make room, and let him stand before our face.
    Shylock, the world thinks—and I think so too—
    That thou but lead'st this fashion of thy malice
    To the last hour of act, and then 'tis thought
    Thou'lt show thy mercy and remorse more strange
    Than is thy strange apparent cruelty,
    And where thou now exacts the penalty—
    Which is a pound of this poor merchant's flesh—
    Thou wilt not only loose the forfeiture,
    But, touched with human gentleness and love,

Forgive a moiety of the principal,
Glancing an eye of pity on his losses,
That have of late so huddled on his back
Enough to press a royal merchant down
And pluck commiseration of his state
From brassy bosoms and rough hearts of flint,
From stubborn Turks and tartars never trained
To offices of tender courtesy.
We all expect a gentle answer, Jew.

SHYLOCK: I have possessed your grace of what I purpose,
And by our holy Sabbath have I sworn
To have the due and forfeit of my bond.
If you deny it, let the danger light
Upon your charter and your city's freedom.
You'll ask me why I rather choose to have
A weight of carrion flesh than to receive
Three thousand ducats. I'll not answer that,
But say it is my humour. Is it answered?
What if my house be troubled with a rat,
And I be pleased to give ten thousand ducats
To have it baned? What, are you answered yet?
Some men there are love not a gaping pig,
Some that are mad if they behold a cat,
And others when the bagpipe sings i'th'nose
Cannot contain their urine; for affection,
Mistress of passion, sways it to the mood
Of what it likes or loathes. Now for your answer:
As there is no firm reason to be rendered
Why he cannot abide a gaping pig,
Why he a harmless necessary cat,
Why he a woolen bagpipe, but of force
Must yield to such inevitable shame
As to offend himself being offended,
So can I give no reason, nor I will not,
More than a lodg'd hate and a certain loathing
I bear Antonio, and I follow thus
A losing suit against him. Are you answered?

BASSANIO: This is no answer, thou unfeeling man,
    To excuse the current of thy cruelty.

SHYLOCK: I am not bound to please thee with my answers.

BASSANIO: Do all men kill the things they do not love?

SHYLOCK: Hates any man the thing he would not kill?

BASSANIO: Every offence is not a hate at first.

SHYLOCK: What, wouldst thou have a serpent sting thee
        twice?

ANTONIO: I pray you think you question with the Jew.
    You may as well go stand upon the beach
    And bid the main flood bate his usual height;
    You may as well use question with the wolf
    Why he hath made the ewe bleat for the lamb;
    You may as well forbid the mountain pines
    To wag their high tops and to make no noise
    When they are fretten with the gusts of heaven,
    You may as well do anything most hard
    As seek to soften that—than which what's harder?—
    His Jewish heart. Therefore, I do beseech you,
    Make no more offers, use no father means.
    But with all brief and plain conveniency
    Let me have judgment and the Jew his will.

BASSANIO: For thy three thousand ducats here is six.

SHYLOCK: If every ducat in six thousand ducats
    Were in six parts, and every part a ducat,
    I would not draw them. I would have my bond.

DUKE: How shalt thou hope for mercy, rend'ring none?

SHYLOCK: What judgment shall I dread, doing no wrong?

*He takes a black actor from the group and shows him to the Court
to illustrate the hypocrisy of Venetian society.*

    You have among you many a purchased slave
    Which, like your asses and your dogs and mules,

You use in abject and in slavish parts
Because you bought them. Shall I say to you
'Let them be free, marry them to your heirs.
Why sweat they under burdens? Let their beds
Be made as soft as yours, and let their palates
Be seasoned with such viands.' You will answer
'The slaves are ours.' So do I answer you.
The pound of flesh which I demand of him
Is dearly bought. 'Tis mine, and I will have it.
If you deny me, fie upon your law:
There is no force in the decrees of Venice.
I stand for judgment. Answer: shall I have it?

DUKE: Upon my power I may dismiss this court
Unless Bellario, a learned doctor
Whom I have sent for to determine this,
Come here today.

SALERIO: My lord, here stays without
A messenger with letters from the doctor,
New come from Padua.

DUKE: Bring us the letters. Call the messenger.

BASSANIO: Good cheer, Antonio. What, man, courage yet!
The Jew shall have my flesh, blood, bones, and all
Ere thou shalt lose for me one drop of blood.

ANTONIO: I am a tainted wether of the flock,
Meetest for death. The weakest kind of fruit
Drops earliest to the ground; and so let me.
You cannot better be employed, Bassanio.
Than to live still and write mine epitaph.

Enter SALERIO with NERISSA (disguised as judge's clerk).

DUKE: Came you from Padua, from Bellario?

NERISSA: From both, my lord. Bellario greets your grace.

BASSANIO: Why dost thou whet thy knife so earnestly?

SHYLOCK: To cut the forfeit from that bankrupt there.

GRAZIANO: Not on thy sole but on thy soul, harsh Jew.
    Thou mak'st thy knife keen. But no metal can,
    No, not the hangman's axe, bear half the keenness
    Of thy sharp envy. Can no prayer pierce thee?

SHYLOCK: No, none that thou hast wit enough to make.

GRAZIANO: O, be thou damned, inexorable dog,
    And for thy life let justice be accused!
    Thou almost mak'st me waver in my faith
    To hold opinion with Pythagoras
    That souls of animals infuse themselves
    Into the trunks of men. Thy currish spirit
    Governed a wolf who, hanged for human slaughter,
    Even from the gallows did his fell soul fleet,
    And, whilst thou lay'st in the unhallowed dam,
    Infused itself in thee; for thy desires
    Are wolvish, bloody, starved, and ravenous.

SHYLOCK: Till thou canst rail the seal from off my bond
    Thou but offend'st thy lungs to speak so loud.
    Repair thy wit, good youth, or it will fall
    To cureless ruin. I stand here for law.

DUKE: This letter from Bellario doth commend
    A young and learned doctor to our court.
    Where is he?

NERISSA: He attended here hard by
    To know your answer, whether you'll admit him.

DUKE: With all my heart. Some three or four of you
    Go give him courteous conduct to this place.
    And here, I take it, is the doctor come.
    Give me your hand. Come you from old Bellario?

PORTIA: I did, my lord.

DUKE: You are welcome. Take your place.
    Are you acquainted with the difference
    That holds this present question in the court?

PORTIA: I am informed thoroughly of the cause.
    Which is the merchant here, and which the Jew?

DUKE: Antonio and old Shylock, both stand forth.

PORTIA: Is your name Shylock?

SHYLOCK: Shylock is my name.

PORTIA: Of a strange nature is the suit you follow.
    Yet in such rule that the Venetian law
    Cannot impugn you as you do proceed.
    You stand within his danger, do you not?

ANTONIO: Ay, so he says.

PORTIA: Do you confess the bond?

ANTONIO: I do.

PORTIA: Then must the Jew be merciful.

SHYLOCK: On what compulsion must I? Tell me that.

PORTIA: The quality of mercy is not strained.
    It droppeth as the gentle rain from heaven
    Upon the place beneath. It is twice blest:
    It blesseth him that gives, and him that takes.
    'Tis mightiest in the mightiest. It becomes
    The throned monarch better than his crown.
    His sceptre shows the force of temporal power,
    The attribute to awe and majesty,
    Wherein doth sit the dread and fear of kings;
    But mercy is above this sceptred sway.
    It is enthroned in the hearts of kings;
    It is an attribute to God himself,
    And earthly power doth then show likest God's
    When mercy seasons justice. Therefore, Jew,
    Though justice be thy plea, consider this:
    That in the course of justice none of us
    Should see salvation. We do pray for mercy,
    And that same prayer doth teach us all to render
    The deeds of mercy. I have spoke thus much

  To mitigate the justice of thy plea,
  Which if thou follow, this strict court of Venice
  Must needs give sentence 'gainst the merchant there.

SHYLOCK: My deeds upon my head! I crave the law,
  The penalty and forfeit of my bond.

PORTIA: Is he not able to discharge the money?

BASSANIO: Yes, here I tender it for him in the court,
  Yea, twice the sum. If that will not suffice
  I will be bound to pay it ten times o'er
  On forfeit of my hands, my head, my heart.
  If this will not suffice, it must appear
  That malice bears down truth. And, I beseech you,
  Wrest once the law to your authority.
  To do a great right, do a little wrong,
  And curb this cruel devil of his will.

PORTIA: It must not be. There is no power in Venice
  Can alter a decree established.
  'Twill be recorded for a precedent,
  And many an error by the same example
  Will rush into the state. It cannot be.

SHYLOCK: A Daniel come to judgment, yea, a Daniel!
  O wise young judge, how I do honour thee!

PORTIA: I pray you let me look upon the bond.

SHYLOCK: Here 'tis, most revered doctor, here it is.

PORTIA: Shylock, there's thrice thy money offered thee.

SHYLOCK: An oath, an oath! I have an oath in heaven.
  Shall I lay perjury upon my soul?
  No, not for Venice. (*He is looking at* JESSICA.)

PORTIA: Why, this bond is forfeit,
  And lawfully by this the Jew may claim
  A pound of flesh, to be by him cut off
  Nearest the merchant's heart. Be merciful.
  Take thrice thy money. Bid me tear the bond.

SHYLOCK: When it is paid according to the tenor.
It doth appear you are a worthy judge.
You know the law. Your exposition
Hath been most sound. I charge you, by the law
Whereof you are a well-deserving pillar,
Proceed to judgment. By my soul I swear
There is no power in the tongue of man
To alter me. I stay here on my bond.

ANTONIO: Most heartily I do beseech the court
To give the judgment.

PORTIA: Why, then thus it is:
You must prepare your bosom for his knife—

SHYLOCK: O noble judge, O excellent young man!

PORTIA: For the intent and purpose of the law
Hath full relation to the penalty
Which here appeareth due upon the bond.

SHYLOCK: 'Tis very true. O wise and upright judge!
How much more elder art thou than thy looks!

PORTIA: Therefore lay bear your bosom.

SHYLOCK: Ay, his breast.
So says the bond, doth it not, noble judge?
'Nearest his heart'—those are the very words.

PORTIA: It is so. Are there balance here
To weigh the flesh?

SHYLOCK: I have them ready.

PORTIA: Have by some surgeon, Shylock, on your charge
To stop his wounds, lest he do bleed to death.

SHYLOCK: Is it so nominated in the bond?

PORTIA: It is not so expressed, but what of that?
'Twere good you do so much for charity.

SHYLOCK: I cannot find it. 'Tis not in the bond.

PORTIA: You, merchant, have you anything to say?

ANTONIO: But little. I am armed and well prepared.
    Give me your hand, Bassanio; fare you well.
    Grieve not that I am fall'n to this for you,
    For herein Fortune shows herself more kind
    Than is her custom; it is still her use
    To let the wretched man outlive his wealth
    To view with hollow eye and wrinkled brow
    An age of poverty, from which ling'ring penance
    Of such misery doth she cut me off.
    Commend me to your honourable wife.
    Tell her the process of Antonio's end.
    Say how I loved you. Speak me fair in death,
    And when the tale is told, bid her be judge
    Whether Bassanio had not once a love.
    Repent but you that you shall lose your friend,
    And he repents not that he pays your debt;
    For if the Jew do cut but deep enough,
    I'll pay it instantly, with all my heart.

BASSANIO: Antonio, I am married to a wife
    Which is as dear to me as life itself,
    But life itself, my wife, and all the world
    Are not with me esteemed above thy life.
    I would lose all, ay, sacrifice them all
    Here to this devil, to deliver you.

PORTIA: (*Aside.*) Your wife would give you little thanks for that
    If she were by to hear you make the offer.

GRAZIANO: I have a wife who, I protest, I love.
    I would she were in heaven so she could
    Entreat some power to change this currish Jew.

NERISSA: (*Aside.*) 'Tis well you offer it behind her back;
    The wish would make an unquiet house.

SHYLOCK: (*Aside.*) These be the Christian husbands. I have a daughter.
    Would any of the stock of Barabbas

> Had been her husband rather than a Christian.
> (*Aloud.*) We trifle time. I pray thee pursue sentence.

PORTIA: A pound of that same merchant's flesh is thine.
The court awards it, and the law doth give it.

SHYLOCK: Most rightful judge!

PORTIA: And you must cut this flesh from his breast.
The law allows it, and the court awards it.

SHYLOCK: Most learned judge! A sentence: come, prepare.

PORTIA: Tarry a little. There is something else.
This bond doth give thee here no jot of blood.
The words expressly are a 'pound of flesh'.
Take then thy bond. Take thou thy pound of flesh.
But in the cutting it, if thou dost shed
One drop of Christian blood, thy lands and goods
Are by the laws of Venice confiscate
Unto the state of Venice.

GRAZIANO: O upright judge!
Mark, Jew! O learned judge!

SHYLOCK: Is that the law?

PORTIA: Thyself shalt see the act;
For as thou urgest justice, be assured
Thou shalt have justice more than thou desir'st.

GRAZIANO: O learned judge! Mark, Jew—a learned judge!

SHYLOCK: I take this offer, then. Pay the bond thrice,
And let the Christian go.

BASSANIO: Here is the money.

PORTIA: Soft,
The Jew shall have all justice. Soft, no haste.
He shall have nothing but the penalty.

GRAZIANO: O Jew, an upright judge, a learned judge!

PORTIA: Therefore prepare thee to cut off the flesh.

> Shed thou no blood, nor cut thou less nor more
> But just a pound of flesh. If thou tak'st more
> Or less than just a pound, be it but so much
> As makes it light or heavy in the substance
> Or the division of the twentieth part
> Of one poor scruple—nay, if the scale do turn
> But in the estimation of a hair,
> Thou diest, and all the goods are confiscate.

GRAZIANO: A second Daniel, a Daniel, Jew!
  Now, infidel, I have you on the hip.

PORTIA: Why doth the Jew pause? Take thy forfeiture.

SHYLOCK: Give me my principal, and let me go.

BASSANIO: I have it ready for thee. Here it is.

PORTIA: He hath refused it in the open court.
  He shall have merely justice and his bond.

GRAZIANO: A Daniel, still say I, a second Daniel!
  I thank thee, Jew, for teaching me that word.

SHYLOCK: Shall I not have barely my principal?

PORTIA: Thou shalt have nothing but the forfeiture
  To be so taken at thy peril, Jew.

SHYLOCK: Why then, the devil give him good of it.
  I'll stay no longer question.

PORTIA: Tarry, Jew.
  The law hath yet another hold on you.
  It is enacted in the laws of Venice,
  If it be proved against an alien
  That by direct or indirect attempts
  He seek the life of any citizen,
  The party 'gainst the which he doth contrive
  Shall seize one half his goods; the other half
  Comes to the privy coffer of the state,
  And the offender's life lies in the mercy
  Of the Duke only, 'gainst all other voice—

In which predicament I say thou stand'st,
For it appears by manifest proceeding
That indirectly, and directly too
Thou hast contrived against the very life
Of the defendant, and thou hast incurred
The danger formerly by me rehearsed.
Down, therefore, and beg mercy of the Duke.

GRAZIANO: Beg that thou mayst have leave to hang thyself—
And yet, thy wealth being forfeit to the state,
Thou hast not left the value of a cord.
Therefore thou must be hanged at the state's charge.

He is swinging a tiny noose.

DUKE: That thou shalt see the difference of our spirit,
I pardon thee thy life before thou ask it.
For half thy wealth, it is Antonio's.
The other half comes to the general state,
Which humbleness may drive unto a fine.

PORTIA: Ay, for the state, not for Antonio.

SHYLOCK: Nay, take my life and all, pardon not that.
You take my house when you do take the prop
That doth sustain my house; you take my life
When you do take the means whereby I live.

PORTIA: What mercy can you render him, Antonio?

GRAZIANO: A halter, gratis. Nothing else, for God's sake.

ANTONIO: So please my lord the Duke and all the court
To quit the fine for one half of his goods,
I am content, so he will let me have
The other have in use, to render it
Upon his death unto the gentleman
That lately stole his daughter.
Two things provided more: that for this favour
He presently become a Christian;
The other, that he do record a gift
Here in the court of all he dies possessed

Unto his son, Lorenzo, and his daughter.

DUKE: He shall do this, or else I do recant
The pardon that I late pronounced here.

PORTIA: Art thou contented, Jew? What dost thou say?

SHYLOCK waits and looks around. He bursts into outrageous laughter at the absurdity of his situation.

SHYLOCK: I am 'content'.

He goes to the DUKE, puts down his yamulka.

PORTIA: Clerk, draw a deed of gift

SHYLOCK: I pray you give me leave to go from hence.
I am not well. Send the deed after me,
And I will sign it.

DUKE: Get thee gone, but do it.

GRAZIANO: In christ'ning shall thou have two godfathers.
Had I been judge thou shouldst have had ten more,
To bring thee to the gallows, not the font.

SHYLOCK leaves. The crowd watch with hostility and then turn on TUBAL. He leaves.

DUKE: Sir, I entreat you home with me to dinner.

PORTIA: I humbly do desire your Grace of pardon.
I must away this night towards Padua,
And it is meet I presently set forth.

DUKE: I am sorry that your leisure serves you not.
Antonio, gratify this gentleman,
For in my mind you are much bound to him.

Exit DUKE.

BASSANIO: Most worthy gentleman, I and my friend
Have by your wisdom been this day acquitted
Of grievous penalties, in lieu whereof
Three thousands ducats due unto the Jew

We freely cope your courteous pains withal.

ANTONIO: And stand in debted over and above
    In love and service to you evermore.

PORTIA: He is well paid that is well satisfied,
    And I, delivering you, am satisfied,
    And therein do account myself well paid.
    My mind was never yet more mercenary.
    I pray you know me when we meet again.
    I wish you well; and so I take my leave.

BASSANIO: Dear sir, of force I must attempt you further.
    Take some remembrance of us as a tribute,
    Not as fee. Grant me two things, I pray you:
    Not to deny me, and to pardon me.

PORTIA: You press me far, and therefore I will yield.
    Give me your gloves. I'll wear them for your sake.
    And for your love I'll take this ring from you.
    Do not draw back your hand. I'll take no more,
    And you in love shall not deny me this.

BASSANIO: This ring, good sir? Alas, it is a trifle.
    I will not shame myself to give you this.

PORTIA: I will have nothing else, but only this;
    And now, methinks, I have a mind to it.

BASSANIO: There's more depends on this than on the value.
    The dearest ring in Venice will I give you,
    And find it out by proclamation.
    Only for this, I pray you pardon me.

PORTIA: That 'scuse serves many men to save their gifts.
    An if your wife be not a madwoman,
    And know how well I have deserved this ring,
    She would not hold our enemy for ever
    For giving it to me. Well, peace be with you.

Exit PORTIA and NERISSA.

ANTONIO: My lord Bassanio, let him have the ring.

Let his deservings and my love withal
Be valued 'gainst your wife's commandment.

BASSANIO: Go, Graziano, run and overtake him.
Give him the ring, and bring him, if thou canst,
Unto Antonio's house. Away, make haste.
Come, you and I will thither presently,
And in the morning early will be both.
Fly towards Belmont. Come, Antonio.

Exit.

SCENE TWENTY
The Ghetto

There are Jews wearing yellow on their clothes

Enter PORTIA and NERISSA (still disguised).

PORTIA sees Jews and shows her distaste.

PORTIA: Enquire the Jew's house out, give him this deed,
And let him sign it. We'll away tonight,
And be a day before our husbands home.
This deed will be well welcome to Lorenzo.

Enter GRAZIANO.

GRAZIANO: Fair sir, you are well o'erta'en.
My Lord Bassanio upon more advice
Hath sent you here this ring, and doth entreat
Your company at dinner.

PORTIA: That cannot be.
His ring I do accept most thankfully,
And so I pray you to tell him. Furthermore,
I pray you show my youth old Shylock's house.

GRAZIANO: That will I do.

NERISSA: Sir, I would speak with you.
I'll see if I can get my husband's ring
Which I did make him swear to keep forever.

PORTIA: Thou mayst; I warrant we shall
　　Have old swearing
　　That they did give the rings away to men.
　　But we'll outface them, and outswear them too.
　　Away, make haste. Thou know'st where I will tarry.

NERISSA: Come, good sir, will you show me to this house?

SCENE TWENTY ONE
Belmont Garden

The playing of the scene reveals deep tension between JESSICA and LORENZO as if they are emerging from a row. This text needs playing with grit rather than romantically.

LORENZO: The moon shines bright. In such a night as this,
　　When the sweet wind did gently kiss the trees
　　And they did make no noise—in such a night
　　Troilus, methinks, mounted the Trojan walls,
　　And sighed his soul towards the Grecian tents
　　Where Cressid lay that night.

JESSICA:　　　　　　　　　In such a night
　　Did Thisbe fearfully o'ertrip the dew
　　And saw the lion's shadow ere himself,
　　And ran dismayed away.

LORENZO:　　　　　　　In such a night,
　　Stood Dido with a willow in her hand
　　Upon the wild sea banks, and waft her love
　　To come again to Carthage.

JESSICA:　　　　　　　In such a night
　　Medea gathered the enchanted herbs
　　That did renew old Aeson.

LORENZO:　　　　　　In such a night
　　Did Jessica steal from the wealthy Jew,
　　And with an unthrift love did run from Venice
　　As far as Belmont.

JESSICA:　　　　In such a night

Did young Lorenzo swear he loved her well,
Stealing her soul with many vows of faith,
And ne'er a true one.

LORENZO: In such a night
Did pretty Jessica, like a little shrew,
Slander her love, and he forgave it her.

Enter STEFANO, a messenger.

Who comes so fast in silence of the night?

STEFANO: Stefano is my name and I bring word
My mistress will before break of day
Be here at Belmont. She doth stray about
By holy crosses where she kneels and prays
For happy wedlock hours
I pray you is my master yet returned?

LORENZO: He is not, nor we have not heard from him.
But go we in, I pray thee, Jessica
And ceremoniously let us prepare
Some welcome for the mistress of the house.
My friend Stefano, signify, I pray you.
Within the house your mistress is at hand,
And bring your music forth into the air,
How sweet the moonlight sleeps upon this bank!
Here will we sit, and let the sounds of music
Creep in our ears. Soft stillness and the night
Become the touches of sweet harmony.
Sit, Jessica.

A sad song from two women.

JESSICA: I am never merry when I hear sweet music.

LORENZO: The reason is your spirits are attentive,
For do but note a wild and wanton herd
Or race of youthful and unhandled colts,
Fetching mad bounds, bellowing and neighing loud,
Which is the hot condition of their blood,
If they but hear perchance a trumpet sound,

> Or any air of music touches their ears,
> You shall perceive them make a mutual stand,
> Their savage eyes turned to a modest gaze
> By the sweet power of music.
> The man that hath no music in himself,
> Nor is not moved with concord of sweet sounds,
> Is fit for treason, stratagems, and spoils.
> The motions of his spirit are dull as night,
> And his affections dark as Erebus.
> Let no such man be trusted. Mark the music.

Enter PORTIA and NERISSA.

PORTIA: That light we see is burning in my hall.
How far that little candle throws his beams—
So shines a good deed in a naughty world.

LORENZO: Dear lady, welcome home.

PORTIA: We have been praying for our husbands' welfare,
Which speed we hope the best for our words.
Are they returned?

LORENZO: Madam, they are not yet,
But there is come a messenger before
To signify their coming.

PORTIA: Go in, Nerissa.
Give order to my servants that they take
No note at all of our being absent hence;
Nor you, Lorenzo; Jessica, nor you.

LORENZO: Your husband is at hand. I hear his trumpet.
We are no tell-tales, madam. Fear you not.

ACTOR: (*With mobile phone.*) Hey guys. Stop! The director's on
the Rialto. She'll be here soon so let's get finished before
she arrives. Double speed. OK?

SARAH: What about Shylock?

ACTOR: We've got to do the happy end.

SARAH: What 'happy end'?

The ensemble now play the text double speed and 'comment' on Shakespeare's easy wind up into a 'happy end'.

PORTIA: This night methinks is but the daylight sick
It looks a little paler, 'tis a day
Such as the day is when the sun is hid.

Enter BASSANIO, ANTONIO, GRAZIANO.

BASSANIO: We should hold day with the Antipodes
If you would walk in absence of the sun.

PORTIA: Let me give light, but let me not be light;
For a light wife doth make a heavy husband,
And never be Bassanio so for me.
But God sort all. You are welcome home, my lord.

BASSANIO: I thank you, madam. Give welcome to my friend.
This is the man, this is Antonio,
To whom I am so infinitely bound.

PORTIA: You should in all sense be much bound to him,
For as I hear he was much bound for you.

ANTONIO: No more than I am well acquitted of.

PORTIA: Sir, you are very welcome to our house.
It must appear in other ways than words,
Therefore I scant this breathing courtesy.

GRAZIANO: By yonder moon I swear you do me wrong.
In faith, I gave it to the judge's clerk.
Would he were gelt that had it for my part,
Since you do take it, love, so much at heart.

PORTIA: A quarrel, ho, already? What's the matter?

GRAZIANO: About a hoop of gold, a paltry ring
That she did give me, whose posy was
For all the world like cutler's poetry
Upon a knife—'love me and leave me not.'

NERISSA: What talk you of this posy or the value?
    You swore to me when I did give it you
    That you would wear it till your hour of death,
    And that it should lie with you in your grave.
    Though not for me, yet for your vehement oaths
    You should have been respective and have kept it.
    Gave it to a judge's clerk?—no, God's my judge,
    The clerk will ne'er wear hair on's face that had it.

GRAZIANO: He will and if he live to be a man.

NERISSA: Ay, if a woman live to be a man.

GRAZIANO: Now by this hand, I gave it to a youth,
    A kind boy, a little scrubbed boy
    No higher than thyself, the judge's clerk,
    A prating boy that begged it as a fee.
    I could not for my heart deny it him.

PORTIA: You were to blame, I must be plain with you,
    To part so slightly with your wife's first gift,
    A thing stuck on with oaths upon your finger,
    And so riveted with faith unto your flesh.
    I gave my love a ring, and made him swear
    Never to part with it; and here he stands.
    I dare be sworn for him would not leave it,
    Nor pluck it from his finger for the wealth
    That the world masters. Now, in faith, Graziano,
    You give your wife too unkind a cause of grief.
    An 'twere to me, I should be mad at it.

BASSANIO: (*Aside.*) Why, I were best to cut my left hand off
    And swear I lost the ring defending it.

GRAZIANO: My lord Bassanio gave his ring away
    Unto the judge that begged it, and indeed
    Deserved it, too, and then the boy his clerk,
    That took some pains in writing, he begged mine,
    And neither man nor master would take aught
    But the two rings.

PORTIA: What ring gave you, my lord?

    Not that, I hope, which you received of me.

BASSANIO: If I could add a lie unto a fault
    I would deny it; but you see my finger
    Hath not the ring upon it. It is gone.

PORTIA: Even so void is your false heart of truth.
    By heaven, I will ne'er come in your bed
    Until I see the ring.

NERISSA: Nor I in yours
    Till I see mine again.

BASSANIO: Sweet Portia,
    If you did know to whom I gave the ring,
    If you did know for whom I gave the ring,
    And would conceive for what I gave the ring,
    And how unwillingly I left the ring
    When naught would be accepted but the ring,
    You would abate the strength of your displeasure.

PORTIA: If you had known the virtue of the ring,
    Or half her worthiness that gave the ring,
    Or your own honour to contain the ring,
    You would not then have parted with the ring.
    I'll die for't but some woman had the ring.

ANTONIO: I am th'unhappy subject of these quarrels.
    I once did lend my body for his wealth
    Which, but for him that had your husband's ring,
    Had quite miscarried. I dare be bound again,
    My soul upon the forfeit, that your lord
    Will never more break faith advisedly.

PORTIA: Then you shall be his surety. Give him this,
    And bid him keep it better than the other.

ANTONIO: Here, lord Bassanio, swear to keep this ring.

BASSANIO: By heaven, it is the same I gave the doctor!

PORTIA: I had it of him. Pardon me, Bassanio,
    For by this ring, the doctor lay with me.

NERISSA: And pardon me, my gentle Graziano,
    For that same scrubbed boy, the doctor's clerk,
    In lieu of this last night did lie with me.

GRAZIANO: Why, this is like the mending of highways
    In summer where the ways are fair enough!
    What, are we cuckolds ere we have deserved it.

PORTIA: Speak not so grossly. You are all amazed.
    Here is a letter. Read it at your leisure.
    It comes from Padua, from Bellario.
    There you shall find that Portia was the doctor,
    Nerissa there her clerk. Lorenzo here
    Shall witness I set forth as soon as you,
    And even but now returned. I have not yet
    Entered my house. Antonio, you are welcome,
    And I have better news in store for you
    Than you expect. Unseal this letter soon.
    There you shall find three of your argosies
    Are richly come to harbour suddenly.
    You shall not know by what strange accident
    I chanced on this letter.

ANTONIO: I am dumb!

BASSANIO: Were you the doctor and I knew you not?

GRAZIANO: Where you the clerk that is to make me cuckold?

NERISSA: Ay, but the clerk that never means to do it
    Unless he live until he be a man.

BASSANIO: Sweet doctor, you shall be my bedfellow.
    When I am absent, then lie with my wife.

ANTONIO: Sweet lady, you have given my life and living.
    For here I read for certain that my ships
    Are safely come to shore.

PORTIA: How now, Lorenzo?
    My clerk hath some good comforts, too, for you.

NERISSA: Ay, and I'll give them him without a fee.

There do I give to you and Jessica
From the rich Jew a special deed of gift,
After his death, of all he dies possessed of.

LORENZO: Fair ladies, you drop manna in the way
Of starved people.

PORTIA: It is almost morning,
And yet I am sure you are not satisfied
Of these events at full. Let us go in,
And charge us there upon inter'gatories,
And we will answer all things faithfully.

GRAZIANO: Let it be so. The first inter'gatory
That my Nerissa shall be sworn on is
Whether till the next night she had rather stay,
Or go to bed now, being two hours to day.
But were the day come, I should wish it dark
Till I were couching with the doctor's clerk.
Well, while I live I'll fear no other thing
So sore as keeping safe Nerissa's ring.

SCENE TWENTY TWO
The Street

SHYLOCK is forcibly converted with his back on a plank.

INQUISITOR: Satan is the king of the Jews. Say after me. 'I
believe in Jesus. He is the Son of God'.

*Silence. SHYLOCK says the Shema in Hebrew to try and drown out
the Inquisitor's conversion.*

Accept Christ or die on the rack tonight. I baptise you in
the name of the Father, the Son and the Holy Ghost!

Shylock is now a Christian!

Silence.

Plank drops.

SCENE TWENTY THREE

SHYLOCK is left alone onstage. SARAH enters. They cross and acknowledge one another.

SARAH is now alone. VALENTINA enters.

VALENTINA: The water level has dropped. The group is on its way. The tour of the Venice Ghetto starts now. Are you ready?

Blackout.

Sound of carnival offstage brings everone on for a dance and a bow.

End.